To Kluma,

Nú ké aloha pumehana,

Stephen

Change We Must

Change We Must

My Spiritual Journey

Nana Veary

Institute of Zen Studies
Honolulu, Hawaii

NANA VEARY:

CHANGE WE MUST, MY SPIRITUAL JOURNEY

Copyright © 1989 by the Institute of Zen Studies

Photographs copyright © 1989 by Franco Salmoiraghi

Sixth printing, January 2000

Institute of Zen Studies
Honolulu, Hawaii
ISBN 1-877982-06-7

Photographs by Franco Salmoiraghi
Edited by Jocelyn Fujii, Mike Sayama, and Nelson Foster
Hawaiian language editing by Fred Meinecke
Design by Bud Linschoten
Typesetting by Presentations, Inc.

*To the memory of my
grandparents and my mother.
They taught me reverence
for life.*

From the highest peak of my consciousness
I look down upon the nothingness of things and
see instead the beauty of God in all,
for He is all

Contents

Acknowledgments

I would not have dared to write this book without the love of my students. I would like to thank three of them especially: Stephen Long for his encouragement, Jocelyn Fujii for her understanding and long hours of research, and Mike Sayama, whose tireless efforts and patience made this book possible. I feel that Jocelyn and Mike were co-authors with me. I would also like to thank Franco Salmoiraghi, whose pictures add another dimension to this book, and all my family and friends who contributed so generously to this project.

I can never repay them for their unselfish support. I only hope that in some small way the message of this book will help someone who is searching for Truth to realize that we really are spiritual beings.

…It is now December 1999 and time to update these acknowledgements. Nana died in 1993 but her spirit certainly lives on as her book continues to touch people from around the world. With the generous assistance of three foundations here in Honolulu, we are pleased to bring out this fresh edition to mark the tenth anniversary of the first printing and to honor all that Nana represents. We are grateful for the ongoing friendship of the Veary family members and would like to thank the trustees of the Atherton Family Foundation, the Cooke Foundation, and the Hawaii Community Foundation for their support. JoAnn Yamada of the Hawaii Community Foundation provided invaluable assistance in facilitating this support. (Gordon Greene, writing as Director of Publications for the Institute of Zen Studies).

Foreword

All of life can be divided into space, time, and energy. Yagyu Tajima no Kami, a famous Japanese swordmaster, said, "The world of *ki* (vital energy) is very broad." The Hawaiian tradition also emphasized the area of energy or *mana*. This world can be sensed but not seen; it can be felt but is not explicit. Neither, however, is it mystical or esoteric. Most people can relate only to the world they can touch, but the Hawaiians have a certain sensitivity, an intuitive sense of feel, probably from being a sea-faring people. Nana Veary comes from this tradition.

She has an intuitive grasp of the oneness of the universe and is at home in the world of energy. Because of this, although I come from a Japanese tradition, Nana and I speak the same language. We can tune ourselves into the same wavelength and communicate as if we have the same mind.

Nana cannot be measured just by her words. Her presence is most important. When those of us who have been honored to know her read her book, the words will have an added meaning. Others perhaps can sense this presence from the pictures or from reading her book many times. It is through a sense of her state of being that we enter into her spirituality.

Nana has reached people in many spheres of life, and her teachings will bear fruit in society for years to come. Only the tip of her contribution to the world is visible now. Like an iceberg, that which is not seen is huge.

She moves people deeply because she is one with them. For example, though they just met, she touched the life of the artist Kauila Clark. Meeting her led him to think about being Hawaiian and, simultaneously, a universal person in the world of art.

You cannot forget a person like Nana; she stays with you. Someday something will trigger what she said to you, and her words will give you a deeper insight into your life.

Tanouye Tenshin Roshi
Archbishop of Chozen-ji, International Zen Dojo

Introduction

Even in her eighties Nana Veary blossoms. Her posture is erect, her silver hair striking. Her eyes are clear and luminous; her expressions fluid, open, and engaging. Whether merrily drinking sake and eating sushi, meditating, teaching, or even shyly posing for the pictures in this book, Nana radiates a joyous spirituality.

She embodies the spirit of Hotei, the old barefooted, bare-chested, pot-bellied monk who enters the marketplace with bliss-bestowing hands. In Hotei, Zen training has ripened into a life of freedom and light. Smiling broadly, carrying a gourd of sake, Hotei mingles with everyone, does what he pleases, and without saying a word, turns all into Buddhas. Nana is like this, only she uses bliss-bestowing hugs. As she takes you to her heart and squeezes away your constricted sense of self, you lose your suffering in the love that she is.

Beautiful in its simplicity, *Change We Must* presents a life untarnished by pettiness and unwaveringly devoted to the search for truth. If she wanted, Nana could tell a tale of royalty and riches, of power and romance, but these are the incidentals of her life. For her, its substance is the truth that all is God and God is love. In *Change We Must* Nana describes a vision of humanity which transcends our differences and embraces our divinity.

Change We Must has the power to uplift those who are suffering. Jocelyn Fujii had this experience while it was still an unfinished manuscript.

Not long ago, I visited a friend who was seriously ill in a Los Angeles hospital. I took the manuscript of this book with me, thinking that it might comfort my friend, who also loved Nana and Hawai'i.

When I arrived at the hospital, he had just been taken off the respirator following his third major surgery in five days. He was in pain and hallucinating from the operations, anesthetics, and confinement in the intensive care unit. His girlfriend and I took shifts by his bedside because the nurses couldn't reach him.

In his eyes I could see torture and his consciousness struggling to find an anchor and come home. As I sat with him through the night, I read him passages from this book. With each passage I could see the light of recognition flicker in and out of his eyes. As Nana's message of love and reverence opened his heart and dispelled his fear, tears came into his eyes. At 3 or 4 in the morning when there was little to hold on to, Nana's words guided him home.

Several days later, still weak but able to speak, my friend asked me to let his mother read it. His mother felt extremely fragile but was trying to be strong for her son. She was reaching out for hope and understanding. She carted this manuscript around the hospital for days, reading it at every turn so she would be finished by the time I came home. When she had read it, she told me, "This was perfect. It gave me strength when I most needed it."

When I brought the manuscript home, it was dog-eared. It had already made a huge difference in several people's lives.

Mike Sayama, Ph.D.
Director, Institute of Zen Studies

Nana with Hotei

My Hawai'i

'Ea mai Hawai'i Nui Ākea,
'Ea mai loko, mai loko mai o ka pō
Puka mai ka moku, ka 'āina
Ka lālani 'āina o Nu'umea... .

Then rose Hawai'i from the space of time
Arose from inside, from the inner darkness,
Then appeared the island, the land
The row of the islands of Nu'umea... .

S o chanted Ka'upena Wong on March 12, 1988, at my 80th birthday. At a large gathering in my daughter's home, his deep and haunting voice called to the present our Hawaiian past. There was power in this ancient genealogical chant, as if the entire past of my family, of the entire Hawaiian race, were called into the room. The opening lines of this chant, as given by the historian Kahakuikamoana, recount the origin of each of the Hawaiian islands. They tell of the ancestral beings connected with each island, their peopling by the first Hawaiians, and the generations that came after them.

During Ka'upena's chant, every member of my family cried, from my daughters and grandchildren to my great-grandchildren, the youngest of whom was only six months old. The young ones cried audibly, their parents wept silently, but all of us cried, moved by some deep force. I understood the chant and my family's place in the genealogy, but no one else did. Yet we were all moved to tears by the same force.

Counting my long-deceased mother, whose presence I felt strongly, there were five generations of us in the room. The last time I heard that chant I was about seven years old. I remembered my mother performing that chant, and I heard her voice in Ka'upena's that day. When it was over, I looked around at all the different people gathered—old Hawaiians and little children, community leaders and movie stars, businessmen and young people looking like punk rockers. I smiled, realizing that here, in 1988, we were celebrating our heritage in the form of a great-grandmother's birthday, united by a common thread that reached back to the very beginnings of Hawai'i.

I am pure Hawaiian and grew up in a Hawai'i of another era, a place that was entirely different from what we know today. Life was simpler and its rhythm was more natural. I was lucky to be taught and raised according to the old Hawaiian ways. My Hawaiian upbringing, the influence of my parents and grandparents, has sustained me through a long life that has spanned most of the 20th century. In my 80 years, I have managed to combine the life of a modern-day householder with the wanderings of a spiritual seeker. I raised three children, became grandmother to ten and great-grandmother to eight, studied with a *kahuna* (Hawaiian teacher), meditated with a guru, climbed Mount Fuji, studied metaphysics, prayed as a Christian, and sat long hours in Zen meditation, all in my search for truth.

Finally, after years of searching, I have come home. I hope to share my journey with you. I should warn you, however, that I skip the details of my personal life and offer you, instead, the truths that I treasure as I reflect upon my life.

I was born in 1908 on O'ahu and was raised as the foster daughter of a pure Hawaiian mother and a Scots father. Both spoke fluent Hawaiian. He was an atheist; she was a devout Christian who felt a reverence for life and an appreciation for nature that were mainstays of Hawaiian culture. I was named Hannah Lihilihipuamelekule, after the marigolds in my grandmother's garden. Lihilihipuamelekule means "the lacy petals of the marigold blossoms."

From the beginning, I was a loner, an orphan. My natural father died while my mother was pregnant with me. My birth was registered under Kualaku, the name of my foster mother's husband. My mother's foster mother took care of both of us. When I was four and a half years old, my mother died, and my foster grandmother took over raising me. From this point on in the story, I shall refer to her as my mother.

In the old Hawaiian culture, if someone, especially a young person, said, "I want that baby," there were no *if's*, *and's*, or *but's*. You got that baby, even if you were a stranger. That is the Hawaiian *'ohana* (family) style, the *hānai* method of child-rearing. There was no such thing as an unwanted baby. Every child was loved. So it was that my foster mother, Mary, said she wanted me and became my mother upon the early death of my natural mother.

I grew up in Pālama, near downtown Honolulu on the island of O'ahu. Throughout my childhood, the influence of my grandparents was strong. They were, like the older Hawaiians of their day, extremely dignified and spiritually aware. My grandfather was a fisherman and a *kahuna kālaiwa'a*, a canoe-builder. He and my grandmother lived at the entrance to Pearl Harbor in a fishing village called Pu'uloa. We looked forward to visiting them every weekend in their little grass hut.

One day while I was there, children of the village who had been playing in front of the house called out to my grandmother, *"Ē kupuna, he malihini kēia e hō'ea maila."* Grandmother, there is a stranger coming. My grandmother responded, *"Ke hiki mai ka malihini, kāhea mai ia'u."* When he arrives, call me.

When he arrived, the children called, *"Ē kupuna, ua hō'ea maila."* He has arrived. My grandmother came, stood on the *lānai*, and said to the stranger, *"Ē komo mai, kipa mai e pā'ina."* Come in and dine.

While they were eating, I sat on the floor of the *lānai* to eavesdrop. When he was through eating, the visitor thanked my grandmother, and she came forward with a little *puniu*, a coconut dish with salt in it. She extended her hand, and he picked three lumps of salt, put them in his mouth, and went off. When the stranger left, I asked my grandmother if she knew him.

"'A'ole," she said. *"He malihini ho'i."* No, he was a *malihini*. When I asked her why she fed him, she got angry, ordered me to sit on the floor in front of her, and said, "I want you to remember these words for as long as you live, and never forget them: *'A'ole au i hānai aku nei i ke kanaka; akā hānai aku nei au i ka 'uhane a ke Akua i loko ona."* I was not feeding the man; I was entertaining the spirit of God within him.

I was six years old when this happened, and I have never forgotten my grandmother's words. This practice of honoring the other was so much a part of the culture that it needed no name. Today we call it the "aloha spirit," but to the Hawaiians of old it was inherent and natural. They lived it. To feed a stranger passing by—that is pure aloha. Today we have to be taught it because we are so far removed from the Hawaiian culture. And we have given it a name.

"*Alo*" means the bosom, the center of the universe. "*Hā*" is the breath of God. The word is imbued with a great deal of power. I do not use the word casually. Aloha is a feeling, a recognition of the divine. It is not just a word or greeting. When you say "aloha" to someone, you are conveying or bestowing this feeling.

In the Hawai'i of my childhood, this feeling bonded the entire community. The whole village was your family; their sorrows became yours and yours, theirs. We felt we were all related and could not help loving one another. As a child, I called our neighbors "uncle" or "tūtū" or "auntie," a practice still observed by Hawaiian families today. We called it a calabash relationship, a word derived from the tradition we had of always sharing a great big calabash of *poi* that everybody dipped into, strangers and all. Eating from the same bowl, the same calabash—that is aloha.

In most written accounts of old Hawai'i, this inherent spirit of giving and respect is overshadowed by stories of warring chiefs and human sacrifice. In every culture, from Asia to Christendom to our 20th century America in Vietnam and Central America, the warlike aspect of human nature has reared its head and claimed its toll in lives. The Hawaiians were no different. Led by the royalty and chiefs, they did, indeed, wage war.

Yet the underlying nature of the Hawaiian has always been gentle and strong in spirituality. These qualities were inherent in their culture, expressed in their everyday lives—in how they greeted strangers and revered their gods, in how they gave away everything, from food to land and even children. When the villagers went fishing, they distributed their catch all along the coast as long as the fish would last. When those of the neighboring village went fishing, they did the same. The fishing code for the Hawaiians was and still is: Don't take what you want; take only what you need. When there is excess, throw it back or give it away.

When people visited my grandparents, they went home with cooked taro or *poi* and a jar full of *limu* (seaweed) and salt, dried fish or dried *he'e* (octopus). Pearl Harbor in those days had lobsters and was even noted for oysters with pearls. When ships were drydocked, the Hawaiians picked the *pipipi* (mollusks) from the bottom of the ship. In the gardens grew bananas and avocados and guava, which we bartered or gave away. From the land and sea came an abundance that was shared and appreciated.

My grandmother's words about feeding the stranger expressed the basic Hawaiian ethic—a firm belief in human spirituality. Although the Hawaiians felt that their *'aumākua* (personal spirits or family guardians) were forms outside of themselves, they also felt their presence within. The word itself, meaning "my father," encouraged this awareness. It was an unconscious knowing that prompted them to honor and respect "something" within people—the human spirit. So they treated even strangers with reverence. My Hawaiian relatives used to say, *"'A'ole 'oe e 'ike i nā po'opo'o o ha'i."* In other words, "Don't judge others. You don't know their spiritual background."

Rich in metaphor, the Hawaiian language was melodious and graceful like the people. The Hawaiians said, *"He nane kā 'olelo."* The language is a riddle. Before the missionaries came and converted the language into the written word, the Hawaiians used figures of speech in language that was like poetry.

I was fortunate to be taught to speak Hawaiian in the old way. My mother taught me to speak the language softly, without saying anything negative or elaborating. "Leave the details out," she said, "and speak softly." We learned that way because my grandparents were stubborn. They did not want to change the Hawaiian language, so they spoke in idioms. All the ancient chants are in idioms, but today there is virtually nobody, not even those fluent in Hawaiian, who speaks that way.

One day at my grandparents', I was watching my grandmother quilting on the *lānai* while my grandfather raked leaves in the yard. My grandmother said to me, "I don't hear the rake. Go to the railing and see what your grandfather is doing." I saw him leaning on the rake, looking at a group of girls passing by. I reported this to my grandmother.

After awhile, she went up behind him and said softly, *"E nānā ana 'oe iā wai?"* Who are you looking at? Startled, he said, *"E nānā ana ho'i au, i ka māla pua e mā'alo ala."* I was looking at a garden of flowers passing by.

Thus their daily conversations mingled poetry and metaphors in beautiful imagery. Another time, when my grandfather and I were walking along the beach, a little boy came running after us, saying, *"Ē kupuna, kali mai ia'u."* Grandfather, wait for me! Finally he caught up with us and walked along until he said, *"Ē kupuna, make wai 'ia au."* Grandfather, I am thirsty. Grandfather said, *"He pūnāwai kau i ka lewa,"* figuratively referring to a coconut as a fountain of water hanging in the air. The little boy understood the metaphor and, without a word, climbed a nearby coconut tree, gathered some coconuts, broke them open, and drank happily of their water.

This use of the language vanished long ago. Hawaiians today speak the missionary language, a literal type of Hawaiian. The riddle is gone. This is tragic, for when you lose the language, you lose your identity. In all my trips around the world during the 1950s, I found that Hawai'i was the only place where the native language is no longer spoken. When you land in Japan, Japanese is spoken. When you land in France, French is spoken. The Hawaiians have nothing, nothing but aloha, and even that they have to re-learn.

Sometime around 1930, we lived briefly on Maui. A Hawaiian girl that I knew invited me to visit her parents up in Kula. When we arrived, I said *"Hui! 'Auhea ka po'e o kēia hale?"* Where are the people of this house? The man who came out, the father, said in English, "Come up, come up!" I remember that so well: I spoke in Hawaiian to him, and he answered me in English. His wife came out and said, *"Komo mai."* Then she said in English, "Eat!" They were pure Hawaiians, but even way back in the 1930s they could not speak Hawaiian. It is sad because the language is beautiful, and what has been lost can never be replaced.

Dew on Taro

Reverence for Life

The Hawaiian language and way of life may be gone, but the spiritual awareness of the Hawaiian culture can still be remembered and practiced. The Hawaiian religion, which I call "kahunaism," is a philosophy of everyday life. Stripped of ritual, it is pure metaphysics. The essence of kahunaism is a deep and genuine reverence for life—living and becoming a part of everything around you. This is what metaphysics teaches and how the Hawaiians lived.

Watching my grandmother serve the stranger taught me the basic law of the Hawaiian cosmology: we live in a spiritual universe governed by spiritual laws. The Hawaiians knew that they were more than physical beings. Prayers and chants acknowledged the divinity within all things and people. Hawaiians felt a need to touch their Creator, and by some deep inner spirituality, they were able to discover the unity of all life. They were able then to see the big picture, the larger universe that embraced the rocks, the ocean, the birds, the land, the plants, the mountains, and the people. They saw that energy unites all of them.

The Hawaiian word *lōkahi* (unity, harmony) acknowledges the three major forces of God, nature, and humans. The old Hawaiians knew that these forces were related and must be kept in harmony. An understanding of *lōkahi* prompted the Hawaiians to honor their fishing gods, plant by the moon, and conduct all of their daily affairs in accordance with nature. It was not something you could read about and learn; it was passed on by the *kūpuna* (elders) through practice and an inner knowing. Growing up with this, I learned that we can never—and should never attempt to—intellectualize the truth. Truth is simple, and no one knew this better than the Hawaiians.

We had a saying: "*Mai pa'i 'oe i ka po'o o ha'i*". Don't slap another's head. Why? Because we believe the head is the throne of God. We were taught that when we were children. One Thanksgiving when I was a teenager, I brought some friends home from school for the holiday. Like silly little girls, we stayed up late in bed talking, giggling, and gossiping. My mother, who did not speak English but could understand it a little, happened to overhear our conversation and realized that we were gossiping about someone. After breakfast, she said, "May I talk with you privately?" When we went to the lanai, she asked what we were talking about. "Oh, we were just talking about a girl in school," I answered. Never one to get angry, she looked at me quietly, then told me that I must not judge people or criticize them because there is the spirit of God residing in everyone.

My mother lived that truth every day of her life. A devout Congregationalist, she combined the best of Christianity with the ancient Hawaiian ways. She was liberal in her approach to Christianity, absorbing and applying only that which seemed right to her. She lived every day of her life as a Christian, but she also talked to the plants and trees, chanted to the ocean and rocks. She said that when you really listen, you will find that the trees talk, the ocean talks, the rocks talk. It happens telepathically; you hear them in your inner self. I did not understand this at the time, but it all came back to me later in life. My subconscious mind held it for me until I could understand.

Although the Scriptures did not say she should plant with the moon, she planted according to its phases. She taught me to plant root vegetables, such as sweet potatoes, at a certain phase of the moon and flowers at another. She had a great garden. When she planted calladiums, all of a sudden, very quickly, sprouts would appear. My calladiums were dwarfed by hers, so I observed, "Your plant grew up and my plant grew down." My mother said, "You have a deeper understanding in life because you want to go to the roots."

One day when I was seven or eight years old, I took a walk in my mother's beautiful rose garden and learned a big lesson. As children do, I was casually tearing the petals off the blossoms. I had a great time, and when I was through, my mother called me to her. I went to her, and she started pulling my ears and hair. I said, "What did I do?" and she answered, "Did you know that the roses you plucked from the bush and the petals you threw away have feelings just like you? Every time you pull a petal, it cries. This you must not do. Flowers have feelings just like you, and you are not to pluck any flowers unless you are going to use them." From that day on, I have never picked a flower unless I was going to use it, and even then, I always ask permission of the bush. Asking permission before entering the wilderness, picking an herb, or intruding upon nature in any way is part of Hawaiian protocol. When you ask permission of nature and give thanks for its bounty, you are acknowledging spirit in all things and practicing a reverence for life.

My mother not only revered all of life; she practiced what I consider the secret of the power of kahunaism—silence. Silence allows you to tap the source of your being, the still, all-knowing center. There is a direct relationship between silence and metaphysics; you have to go into the silence to practice meditation and other metaphysical methods.

Without knowing it, my mother and grandparents were consummate metaphysicians. They went deep into the silence, using their minds to project their thoughts. My mother told me time and again, "Be silent and observe," and in their presence people just could not help but be quiet. Because they were tranquil and highly spiritual, others became more spiritually attuned in their presence.

My grandparents often repeated the phrase *"Pa'a ka waha, hana ka lima"* while we were growing up: Work with your hands and don't talk. They often cautioned, "You waste your energy talking." Practicing that belief, they did not dissipate their energy with idle chatter, and their words carried power whenever they spoke. They spoke with nature and the elements as naturally as with people.

One day my mother set a beautiful table outside under a tent so she could serve lunch to her friends. With the guests due to arrive in a few minutes and a Hawaiian feast ready to serve, she went to the far corner of the yard, looked up at the dark clouds in the sky, and had a private conversation with them. Very humbly and lovingly, she said, "I am going to have a luncheon here. Please, I don't want to be rude, but please, will you move to the next valley, and when our luncheon is over, you can come back and rain?" My father, an atheist, looked up at the clearing skies saying, "That wasn't her. The rain had to move." But as soon as the luncheon was over, it poured.

The Hawaiians had the knowledge to work with the elements, but they had to be genuinely humble. Belief and knowledge were important, but they had to be humble above all. When my mother asked the rain to leave our valley, she held the attitude of complete reverence. When she chanted to the ocean, she was offering a prayer to the gods.

When she fished, she waded out into the ocean in her *mu'umu'u* (a loose Hawaiian dress) and patted the water like a child, chanting all the while. Fish came to her, and she lifted the hem of her *muʻumuʻu* to form a net. The fish actually jumped into it! She usually threw all but two *manini* (surgeon fish) back into the ocean according to the fishermen's code: Take only what you need and not what you want.

My mother also had a pet shark out near the entrance to Pearl Harbor, where my grandparents lived. Every time her father went fishing, he came home with a canoe full of fish for the village. Some of the catch always went to Kaʻahupāhau, her shark, which she raised from when it was small until it reached over 25 feet in length. Offering the fish to her pet, she chanted, calling Kaʻahupāhau from its den to receive them. Occasionally when it did not respond, my mother dove down to the shark's den, straddled its back, and rode it. It carried her great distances. While all the other villagers worshipped that shark, my mother treated it as a pet.

As I grew older, I came to realize that when you sustain a reverence for life, life responds to you in the same way. Nature responded to my mother and grandparents because they acknowledged its spirit and revered its many forms.

My mother was the first Christian in my entire family lineage, but she did not deny kahunaism as she knew it. She was an exception in her ability to practice the two religions without inner conflict. Queen Kaʻahumanu, queen regent of Kamehameha the Great who united the Hawaiian islands, utterly rejected her native religion and converted to Christianity when the missionaries came in 1820. Many others did the same.

A story repeated in my family concerned the well-known prophecy of Hewahewa, Kamehameha's *kahuna*, that the gods of Hawaiʻi would leave them because of abuse and misuse of power. "Our gods are going to leave us, but they shall return between two tapa cloths," Hewahewa said. When the missionaries came with the

Bible, we believe that represented the return of the gods between two tapa cloths. I feel that the same God the Hawaiians had worshipped in the past came back to us through Christianity.

Because I grew up in this rich religious environment, I had a spiritual life even as a young child. When I was five, I accompanied my mother to Congregational "cottage meetings." The meetings were conducted in Hawaiian, and though I was always the only child there, I loved them. That is when I lived in song. People would pray, sing, and testify to their faith. I heard the songs deep within me.

The Hawaiians' great skill as healers also stemmed from their reverence for life. They believed that the body could not respond to any kind of treatment without first being healed mentally and spiritually. Hawaiians always began the process with *ho'oponopono,* a process of putting things right with the whole person. Whenever anyone in the family was in trouble or ill, the senior member of the family gathered everyone together and led them all through this process of restitution and forgiveness. What is most important in *ho'oponopono* is getting right with God. When you are right with God, you are right with your fellow man, and the pressures, tensions, and guilt causing the illness are released. When I was little, if any of the children fell ill, my parents and grandparents gathered, and my grandmother would ask my parents, "What's wrong with the children? Is there something wrong? What have you done?" They believed that, no matter what the condition, the healing could only come with the complete forgiveness of the whole family. The forgiveness must encompass any mistakes or abuses that might have contributed to the condition.

Depending on how large a Hawaiian family was, members would gather for *hoʻoponopono* two or three deep, all in one room. Everything had to be brought out in *hoʻoponopono* because the Hawaiians believe that every word has power. When someone said something unpleasant to a Hawaiian, he would respond, *"Hoʻi nō kāu ʻōlelo me ʻoe."* Your words go back and roost on you. You said that to protect yourself and release it. Otherwise, your subconscious mind would accept it. When you respond in this way, you are not accepting the curse but are releasing it. *Hoʻoponopono* employs this power of the word to release sickness.

A lot of people think that *hoʻoponopono* is pointing out people's faults. It is not that at all. It is forgiving one another. Everybody forgives, and no one is spared forgiveness. If I did something to another, I ask forgiveness. If someone did something to me, he asks me to forgive him. Nobody is above asking forgiveness, no matter who they are or how spiritual they are. Everyone is forgiven because no one is more spiritual than anyone else. Everyone is equal. With *hoʻoponopono*, everyone comes together for a meeting of the minds on the spiritual level. It is not to focus on your thinking or your habits or your faults; it is just releasing your mistakes without arguing. It is asking, "With all the things I've said, thought, and done to you, I ask you to forgive me." You have to ask sincerely, "Please forgive me in thought, word, and deed if I've done anything to hurt you." But you have to mean it. That is all there is to it.

In *hoʻoponopono*, it was usually only the immediate family that gathered to help in the healing. They started with a confession of sorts, a discussion of the mistakes in the presence of the person who was ill. One would turn around and say, "You know, I harbored all sorts of thoughts about you, and I really didn't like you." The sick person must forgive each one in the family. Metaphysically, we are asking God in each person to forgive us. This is what the Hawaiians did. *"ʻAʻole oe i ʻike ka po'opo'o o ha'i,"* they said. In other words, you have not realized my spiritual depth. We are all spirit.

At the same time, the Hawaiians would say, *"Mai kaula'i wale i ka iwi o nā kūpuna."* Don't advertise what's wrong with the family. Even in *ho'oponopono*, the Hawaiians used words sparingly. They would not elaborate on their mistakes in great detail; they would keep it simple and not get tangled up in words. That was very Hawaiian.

Once the *ho'oponopono* was conducted, it was felt the herbs and prayer could take effect. But forgiveness and the involvement of the entire family were necessary in the healing process. Today I recommend meditating twice a day as your own kind of *ho'oponopono*: once in the morning to give thanks to the source, once in the evening to ask forgiveness. This cleanses your life daily and nurtures a reverence for life.

38

Working with Nature

The only problem facing you in life is
your belief in separation from the Source.
Solve that one, and all the others will vanish.

Whom my mother scolded me about wantonly plucking flowers, she was teaching me the attitude necessary for working closely with nature. The Hawaiians lived and worked with nature every day of their lives. From planting to fishing to healing with herbs, they called upon their inner wisdom to make the most of nature's offerings.

In my grandparents' village, the whole family, children and all, was invited to participate in planting. When they planted sweet potatoes, as many rows were planted as there were children to do the planting. Each child stood at the beginning of a row, facing the sun, with a *lauhala* (pandanus leaf) basket filled with sweet potato slips. The elders chanted and prayed before the planting, which was done for the best results when the moon was waxing rather than waning.

Each child was instructed to recite these words to the sun while planting each sweet potato slip: "*Kanu nei au, aia iā 'oe ka ulu.*" I plant and the growth is yours. Throughout the planting, the children backed away from the sun, being careful not to let their shadows fall on the new plants. We had to move and plant, move and plant, without letting our awareness slip for a moment. When the potatoes appeared, what potatoes! If we planted consciously, the potatoes could be as large as a human head. The elders taught, "When the sun is ascending, everything is growing and energy is growing toward its peak."

When my mother sent us out to collect herbs, she always instructed us to be quiet and gave us a prayer to repeat before picking a single leaf. Ask permission and give thanks—that was the Hawaiian protocol that extended to every aspect of life in nature. If you observe this constantly, you begin to develop an inner silence, a deep strength that comes from having your mind attuned to the universal consciousness that pervades all things.

When people got sick, especially if it was paralysis, they were taken to the ocean while it was still dark, placed in the water, and massaged while the sun came up. Facing the sun, the healers performed both the chant and massage. In three days, that person would walk again. When you think about it, it is good common sense to follow the rhythm of life that way.

When I was about seven or eight years of age, I accompanied my mother to Iwilei when she went to have her eyes treated for cataracts that had almost blinded her. The *kahuna lapaʻau* (medical specialist) we visited was called "Makapaʻa Dan" (literally, "one eye" Dan), for he had only one eye. The *kahuna* greeted us and immediately went to work. He said to me in a mixture of Hawaiian and English, "*Ē pēpē*, there is a *kumu pōpolo* in the yard. *ʻAko mai ʻoe i ʻelima lau o ka poho lima. Before you ʻako, pule ʻoe iā Hina. Me keia oe e pule ai.*" That means, "Baby, there's a tree of *pōpolo* (black nightshade) in the yard. After you pray to Hina, pick five leaves. This is the way we pray to Hina," and he taught me a brief chant:

> *Ē Hina ē, ke ʻako nei au i ka lau o ka pōpolo*
> *I lāʻau hoʻi no kuʻu makuahine*
> *Iā ʻoe ke ola, ʻāmama, ua noa.*

I prayed to Hina that day, and in my later years with the Pentecostal Church, I often thought of this as we went out to pray for the sick. Children's prayers have tremendous power.

On this day with the *kahuna*, I added my prayers to my mother's healing. First she washed her eyes with water in which mashed *pōpolo* leaves had soaked. Then the *kahuna* took a piece of sweet potato vine, made a small loop with the stem, and agitated the cataract by rubbing the stem against the eyeball. Then he took lemon grass and made a loop with a thin blade. With a flick of the wrist, he had the cataract hanging from the loop of grass. My mother enjoyed 20-20 eyesight for the remainder of her life, dying at age 54 without ever wearing glasses.

While Makapaʻa Dan was a medical *kahuna*, my grandfather was a *kahuna kālaiwaʻa.* In Hawaiian society, the *kahuna* were the specialists, those trained in the different disciplines: geology, agriculture, healing, astrology, and so on. They were selected from the ruling class and trained as children according to laws and methods handed down from the beginning. It took two decades to become a fully trained, professional *kahuna.* The requirement was to watch, listen, and learn.

They were trained to conserve the resources and to help advance the knowledge of the people. The *kahuna* lived according to spiritual laws, and they encouraged everyone who came to them to live by the same laws. They believed in the power of prayer: before they planted, they prayed; before they ate, they prayed; they prayed over everything they did. They were always aware of the spiritual part of their nature. The fundamental prayer of the *kahuna* was, "Let that which is unknown become known."

My grandfather taught me a lot about this just by living his life in silence. When the need for a new canoe arose, he went into the silence and fasted for three days to become one with Spirit, his teacher. After three days, he walked into the forest to look for a certain bird, having been instructed during the silence which bird would be his guide. It would select the tree out of which the canoe would be carved.

Once when my grandfather went into the forest, there was no bird to be seen for two days. He finally saw a handsome, large tree and said to himself, "That tree will make a fine canoe." Out of nowhere, a bird flew to the tree and began pecking on its trunk, a sure sign that the tree was infested with termites. My grandfather spent another three days following the bird as it flew from tree to tree. Finally the bird, a species of flycatcher, sang, "*'Elepaio, 'elepaio, 'elepaio,*" communicating to my grandfather that this was the tree for the canoe. Then the bird disappeared. It had accomplished its task.

Next, to cut the tree at its base, my grandfather had to ask permission of the tree. After some time, the tree said to him, "For what purpose would I serve you?" My grandfather said, "*I pōmaika'i nā lāhui kānaka apau.*" For the good of the entire race. Only then could he cut the tree down.

When you learn to read nature in this way, it becomes a great ally, and even what others consider supernatural seems perfectly natural. My mother used to say to me, "If you haven't seen *Hale'ole,* you haven't seen the island of Kaua'i." *Hale'ole* is a mirage; *Hale* means "house" and *'ole* means "not" or "nothing," so *Hale'ole* means "no house."

My mother told me that to see *Hale'ole* is to receive a special welcome from other dimensions. She said that *Hale'ole* was unique to Kaua'i and that only a chosen few ever see it. To see it means the island is speaking personally to you.

About nine years ago, when I was there, at the summit of Kalalau overlooking the

Napali coast, I looked up to the clouds and saw a rainbow at sunrise. The rainbow surrounded a vision, clear as day, of a hut among coconut trees, with chickens and dogs walking around. Then it receded and left me only with the experience of having seen *Hale'ole.*

My mother also said, "You haven't seen the Big Island until you've seen Hōpoe." In Hawaiian mythology, the poet Hōpoe is a friend of Pele's sister and is said to be the originator of the hula, thus being mentioned in many chants. My mother said that only the chosen ones would see Hōpoe as a dancing rock, another mirage. When you see it, you have to dive deep into the water and pay homage to Hōpoe.

Whenever I fly to any other island, I ask permission of its guardian spirits. As the airplane lands, I ask permission to be on the island and to partake of its beauty. Whenever I approach Kaua'i, the only island I travel to regularly, I always see a rainbow or some sign of welcome. I always feel that this is nature speaking directly to me, responding to my reverence.

My mother, of course, had innumerable deep experiences with nature. For her the extraordinary was commonplace. She talked with the plants constantly, and they even tattled to her. Once when she left for a meeting on the Big Island, she entrusted my father and me with the enormous responsibility of watering her garden. She was leaving for two weeks, and my father and I dutifully agreed to water the plants. It was summer vacation. The first day was no problem; I watered the plants. But that was the end of it. All of a sudden, the time had gone by, and my father was saying, "Your mother is coming home tomorrow, and you'd better.... "

"She asked you and me to take care of the plants," I reminded him, "so don't think you'll be spared the harangue." He asked me to turn the spigot on, and we ended up flooding the poor plants.

The next day, when my mother returned, I met her at the gate. At that time, neither my father nor I believed that she could communicate with plants, but I noticed that as she walked slowly up the steps to the house, she seemed to be listening to something. She entered the house, took off her *holokū* (gown), put on a *muʻumuʻu*, and came out and sat in the rocker. All of a sudden, she said, "Well, let's go to bed." I looked at my father and said, "We're spared."

Well, my mother never did believe in spanking children on an empty stomach. If there is going to be a spanking, she said, it should always be on a full stomach. The next morning, after we all had breakfast, my mother asked, "Did you two water my plants?" We quickly answered, "Yes!" My mother said, *"Mai aʻo mai ʻoe i ka hoʻopunipuni."* Don't lie to me. She continued, "The plants said that when I left you watered them one day, and then you soaked them and drowned them night before last!"

I said to myself, "No, no, the plants couldn't have talked to her." My father responded aloud, "Really, Mary, your imagination is running away with you." My mother retorted, "Don't you lie to me! I can hear the plants. They talk to me.... The trees talk to me.... The stones talk to me!"

My mother's allies in nature helped her in healing, too. Since she was able to communicate with nature, she had an uncanny curative power, and other families besides ours called upon her for help. I remember the case of a woman who had recently given birth and whose baby had slept all day, causing the mother's breasts to become engorged. Someone called my mother, and she went over. Not knowing what to do, she went into the silence and prayed. Suddenly she looked at the woman's husband and asked him to find a *noni* (Indian mulberry) leaf. When he returned, she heated the leaf over a kerosene lamp and, when it had wilted, placed it on the woman's breasts. In three minutes, her milk was flowing plentifully.

Later, when I myself was nursing one of my babies, I lost my milk, and my mother went out into the yard, cut a vine from the sweet potato plant, and brought it to me, instructing me to wear it as a lei. I did not know why, but I did it, and in no time at all there was milk to feed the baby and then some.

After a childhood full of such incidents, I could not help but believe in powers beyond the rational mind. I love the way everyday things became extraordinary and extraordinary things became commonplace when the Hawaiians worked with nature.

T*he city inspector involved in turning Waimānalo Gulch into a dump called me to ask for Nana's help. At a site which had once been a* heiau *dedicated to the owl, strange incidents had been occurring. Workers suffered from unusual pains; new equipment kept breaking down without apparent cause; freak accidents happened so frequently that men began to refuse to work in the area.*

Before dawn one morning, I took Nana to the site to make an offering of fruits. As we walked, suddenly she stopped in front of a rock and said, "Who's this!" She said, "This is the rock." She turned and told the people, "You should not be here. You have entered an area which is sacred."

She prayed and started to cry, apparently feeling the abuse the land had suffered. The engineers wanted to move the rock so they could continue the project, but Nana declared that the rock was not ready to be moved. The inspector started to walk back to his car when the engine started by itself. Shocked, he said, "How I going turn the engine off when I get my keys in my hand?" Nana blessed him and another worker with salt water, and we left.

Some time passed, and incidents continued. Two huge birds would fly over and dive down, seemingly attacking workers. Serious, even fatal, car accidents occurred on the road near the site.

Finally we went back to move the rock. The men could not lift it. Prior to this, four men could carry the rock, but now they had to set up planks and reverse a truck into the rock. Nana relocated the rock to the top of a hill overlooking the coast, blessed it, and made an offering. After this the strange events stopped.

Gary Omori

The Rock at Waimānalo Gulch

48

Boundless Faith

I got married in 1927. The first big miracle of my life occurred during my oldest daughter's birth. She looked out at the world and went back inside three times. She did not want to be born. The third time, before she could withdraw, the doctor pulled her out. He held her and slapped her, but nothing happened, so he went over to my mother and said, "I'm sorry your granddaughter is stillborn."

My mother never, never spoke English. This was the first and only time in her life I heard her utter words in English. "Give me the baby," she said. The doctor placed the baby in her hands, and she quietly went into the corner of the room, chanting and praying on the floor. She massaged the baby and continued chanting until she heard a voice telling her in Hawaiian, "Open the baby's mouth and breathe in it three times." This she did, and the baby cried. That sound shot through the room and stymied the doctor, who had just finished writing "stillborn" on the birth certificate. He crossed a line through "stillborn" and wrote in "live birth."

When my mother placed her in my arms, she said in Hawaiian, "Take good care of this baby. You take care of her."

In 1932, my spiritual search began. My father died in May, and I was baptized into the Pentecostal Church on Mother's Day at age 23. Seven months later my mother died. Prompted by these losses, I began to search for meaning, for truth, for something that would provide continuity to the spiritual instruction I was given as a child. The Pentecostal Church influenced me profoundly. It taught me love and the power of faith in healing.

When my youngest daughter was 15, she went suddenly and mysteriously blind in both eyes. She was getting ready to go to California to school. Everything was packed when she woke up the day of her flight and asked me to open the blinds. I said, "My God, it's 9:30!" She said it was dark, and I knew then that she was blind. Her trip postponed, she came down with melancholia and asked me to open the Scriptures and read to her. Pointing blindly to a page for me to read, she got down on her knees to pray. I found that she had pointed to the parable about Jesus healing the blind, a testimony to the will of God.

After 25 spinal injections at Straub Clinic in a period of a year, she regained her sight. In the end, the doctor said that each of her eyes held two sets of pupils, one dead and the other functioning fully.

While she was blind, my daughter nonetheless spent some time in California and there developed a terrible oozing rash behind her knees, caused by an allergy to horses. When I approached the minister of the Pentecostal Church and told her about my daughter's raw, painful rash, she counseled me to buy three handkerchiefs, which I did. The church members blessed them, and I sent them to her with the minister's instructions to pray and sprinkle them with olive oil, then wrap her knees with them. She slept this way overnight, and the rash came off into the handkerchief and left her. Overnight, the skin of her knees healed.

On another occasion my oldest daughter broke her arm. It was literally hanging by the skin, and when I took her to Children's Hospital, the doctor said she probably would have to stay two months in the hospital. I said, "Never." I told him I would

Nana with granddaughter, circa 1957

stay with her whether it was two months, two years, or forever. Going home from the hospital for a moment, I met one of the founders of the church and told her about my daughter's broken arm. She relayed the news, and at our regular Sunday night service, the minister told the congregation, "Sister Nana's daughter is sick, so let's all pray for her." I was at the hospital at nine o'clock that night, during the service, when she said suddenly, "I can hold up my arm." I looked at her and screamed. The nurses came and forbade her to do that, saying her arm would get worse. She said, "No, I can move it." The next morning she went for an x-ray, and all you could see was a pencil-thin line, jagged but clean, everything in place. The doctor was incredulous. Just 24 hours after she was admitted to the hospital, he told us to go home.

It was about this time, when I was in my thirties, that I narrowly escaped being sent to a convalescent home for a lung disorder. The doctor told me my lungs were peppered with holes. I prayed and prayed, and a week later, when I was supposed to go to the home, I got another x-ray. When the doctor looked at it, his eyes grew big and he said, "No! It couldn't be!" I wanted to cry, thinking it had gotten worse, but the doctor said, "Now, I want to know what you did during the week." I said, "I did exactly what you told me—go to sleep, rest, rest a lot." The doctor looked at me and started punching my chest and said, "Well, how do you feel?" I said, "I feel fine." He said, "Well, I want to know: where did you buy this new pair of lungs?" He showed me the new x-ray, and it was perfect, no scar tissue, no holes, nothing.

These are the kinds of miracles I experienced in my spiritual journey. I am not saying things come easily; there is no teaching that will make your life a path of roses. The Pentecostal Church, however, taught me that anything is possible. It gave me a faith so strong it is unshakable. No matter how dismal things may seem, I believe that all things are possible to those who believe and learn to love God within themselves. Only when you turn within and feel God can you begin to see God in others. I had learned this from my Hawaiian elders, but it was the Pentecostal Church that gave me direct experience of the power of prayer and faith. I was in the Pentecostal Church for over ten years before I began a new cycle, in metaphysics.

The Happiest Time

Seek to enjoy and not to possess.

For a period of about six years beginning in 1941, I worked as a lifeguard matron at the War Memorial Natatorium, located at the Diamond Head end of Waikiki. Built as a World War I memorial, the Natatorium was then the country's largest saltwater swimming pool and a favorite spot for a lot of boys from 18 to 21 years of age. There was a war going on, and many young people were at loose ends. These kids used to swim at the Natatorium, go fishing, play basketball, and hang out across the street in Kapi'olani Park. I was in my mid-30s, raising my three children with my husband, and the kids all called me "Ma," Ma Veary. I called them "my boys," and I treated them all as if they were my own sons. One day, the cops picked up a whole bunch of them for vagrancy because a few of the rascal ones were making trouble. Some of them had no home to go to; others only had family way out in the country. When I heard they were in jail, I went there, bailed them out, and took them home with me, all 21 boys! I brought them home to our two-bedroom house in Kapahulu to join my own family of five. I did not give it much thought: it seemed the natural thing to do. My husband thought I was nuts, but his heart was big. Soon he got used to seeing the boys walking around in his clothes. We had boys sleeping on the couches, on the floor, in the yard, all over the place.

Some of those boys were great musicians—Johnny Costello, Richard Kauhi, Jimmy Kaku, Lawrence Pedro, and others. From way off in the distance, you could hear them singing and playing the guitar and *'ukulele*. It's hard to believe some of them are dead now. In those days they would come home to the house and sing, or they would play under the stars at the Natatorium.

George Laikupu, whom we all called Bolo, was one of the boys. We had a swimming team that practiced at the Natatorium, and it was thanks to Bolo that one of the girls on the team went on to compete in the Olympics. Bolo went to see the famous swimming coach, Soichi Sakamoto at the University of Hawaii, to ask if he could take her into training. He did, and it changed her life, but part of the reason she got so good was that Bolo trained her and trained her until she could beat him. George's 65 today, with 6 children, a *hānai* child, and 22 grandchildren.

The landlady lived right in the back of my house, and seeing all these young men sleeping over really bothered her. Eventually she evicted us.

I went down to see the superintendent of the Natatorium and told him what had happened. He asked me why my family was evicted, and I said, "You remember those 21 boys?" His eyes got wide, and he said, "Oh no, Ma Veary, you're really nuts." Then he asked me what we were going to do, and I told him about a friend who had offered to wall in her garage for us to live in. He said, "Forget it."

I said, "Why? Have you found a house?" "Yes," he said, "right here. Right here, at the Natatorium." I said, "You mean to tell me I'm going to move in here?" He said, "That's right, I'm going to fix it." So he fixed up a place next to the women's locker room at the Natatorium. It was a great big room, and when it was fixed, I said to him, "Thank you. I will not move in here unless the boys move with me." The superintendent said, "Oh, God, you can't do that. The cops will come!" I told him that if the cops came, I would tell them that the boys were my sons and that I was working at the Natatorium and living there.

So we moved all those boys into the Natatorium. My husband, my children, the boys—we all lived under the bleachers. When the stars were out and it was nice and balmy, we hauled our pillows, blankets, and mats up on the bleachers and slept there, huddled under blankets beneath the open sky. When it rained, we ran for cover inside.

We washed our clothes in the showers or the ocean and dried them on the bleachers. The boys went surfing and swimming, and when they came home, they took out the *'ukulele* and guitars and played music. We cooked our meals on hot plates or an open fire, and when the boys caught fish, we had a feast!

I think that was the happiest time of my life, really. Did I love those boys! If people were difficult with me, or if it looked like something was wrong, they always asked if they could help. They dropped everything if they thought I needed help.

One day, my son came home and asked me why we were still living there. "I've been home two months now, and we've lived here all that time," he said. "How about looking for a place where we can live like human beings?" That really threw me, so I sat him down and said, "You know, son, until you can appreciate the little things in life—until you can just appreciate what you have here—only then will the gates of heaven open for you, only then will the better things in life come to you." He looked at me and apologized.

Two months later, I received a call from a friend who was renting a beautiful home from her mother for only $40 a month. She came to see me at the Natatorium and told me she was moving to the mainland. "My dad and mother are on the Big Island and I don't think they'll ever come here," she said. "What would you think about moving into my house?" Immediately, I thanked God for opening the door for me. We moved into a place that was far better than the old Kapahulu house. The funny thing is, just about that time, the boys all got jobs. In the space of seven or eight months, they got jobs, they got married, they sort of grew up.

Yet now, at Christmas, you can see their cars parked in front of my house. The boys all come home. At first they came with their wives and children, and now they come with their grandchildren. When they have a baby or a grandchild, they call me. If they want a Hawaiian name for their grandchild, they call me.

The Natatorium years were good years. We had a healthy love toward our fellow man. We found great joy in sharing, and we were free and happy. I have always tried to live that way. Perhaps because I was orphaned at four, I learned early the importance of love.

I was one of the boys who hung around the Natatorium in the 1940s. Ma Veary took us in like her own sons. I had no job. I was hanging around the beach, sleeping at the Natatorium, and Ma Veary just picked me up, and before you knew it, I had a job as a lifeguard at the Royal Hawaiian Hotel.

If I heard anybody was sassing her or anything, I came flying down half the length of Waikiki Beach. Everybody cleared out of the Natatorium. I was so mad I'd wipe anybody out. I used to feel like I could take care of anybody. Maybe they could take care of me too, but I didn't care.

The only who could stop me was Ma. She'd grab my shirt and tell me, "Get back to your station! What're you doing down here?" She used to get after me and called me "Hard-head." When she got mad, her eyes got big and red. She put me up against the wall and nailed me down. I used to be so scared I didn't know what to do.

She was a beautiful woman–a mother and good friend. In our daily lives, Ma watched us and helped us correct ourselves. I had a lot of good blessings through Ma Veary.

George Laikupu

The Metaphysical World

In divine providence, salvation is unnecessary,
but self-discovery is essential. We do not save that
which was lost; we merely discover that
which is always there - our divinity.

In 1947 I went with my daughter to buy sheet music at a music store and there saw a pamphlet for Science of Mind on the magazine rack. I read it with interest but was confused because the terminology was so different from that of the Pentecostal faith. As I read about the universal consciousness and the one mind, I asked myself, "Which is God? Are they talking about God?" I pursued this teaching, though, because it taught that everyone has God within. It seemed wonderful because the teaching did not restrict you from being *you.*

I had left the Pentecostal faith because they believed people had to belong to their church to be saved and accepted literally the passage in Revelations saying that only 144,000 will be saved. I felt that if God created multitudes of people it was ridiculous to think He would save only 144,000. So I left. But I had learned that love is the doorway to faith, and to this day I have a strong faith that all things are possible unto those who love God.

After reading the pamphlet, I joined a Science of Mind study group in town, and several months later I went to Los Angeles to study with world-famous metaphysician Ernest Holmes, the founder of Science of Mind. I first met Dr. Holmes at Science of Mind Headquarters, where he was giving a class. He was a short man with a big head. My father used to say that you needed big feet to support a big brain, but he had small feet.

Dr. Holmes ignored me when I entered the room, so finally somebody said, "I have to introduce you to him." I said, "No, no." But she insisted and took me up to meet him. His handshake was fishy. I said I wanted to study with him, but he said, "Oh, no, the class has already begun." Then he asked me where I was from. When I said Hawai'i, that was the magic word. He really shook hands with me then and agreed to teach a special course for five of us.

Classes started in the morning at 8:15 and went to 2:15 in the afternoon. This program of study lasted two years. His classes were hard to grasp, as a brief quotation demonstrates:

> The basic conception of the Science of Mind is that we live in a spiritual universe governed by spiritual laws. God is in, through, around, and for us....
>
> Without trying to define, without making any attempt to explain, you make the simple statement, 'Mind is. Mind is, and mind is both universal and individual.' That is, it is not only universal and abstract, it is also individual and concrete. The mind personified is the same mind which is universal. This is the perception that Buddha, Jesus, and great spiritual leaders had. They understood that the universe had to be one in order to be at all.

Finding these ideas hard to deal with, I regularly stayed after class, and Dr. Holmes tutored me individually.

During one of our final classes, he walked over to the window and said, "Come here, look out the window, and tell me what you see." We all went and looked out. We saw people walking up and down the sidewalks and traffic going by. After a while he said, "What have you seen?" We answered, "Just people walking up and down. Cars and buses passing by." I told him, "I don't see anything unusual." "How long have you studied with me?" he asked. We said two years. He said, "You haven't learned anything, have you? Come back to the window again." We went back to the window, and just then a group of people passed by on the sidewalk. Dr. Holmes looked out and said, "See? God in so many faces passing by." Then I remembered my grandmother telling me that she was not feeding the stranger but entertaining the gods. I thought to myself, "Oh, my god, metaphysics was right before my nose, and I didn't see it."

After two years of studying Science of Mind with Ernest Holmes, just before I was to take the test for my practitioner's license, I had to come back to Hawai'i because my husband was very ill. I thought, "Oh, boy, there goes two years of studying," but after I returned, Dr. Holmes called another practitioner in Hawai'i and gave her the assignment to get an affirmation from me, a saying of my own that illustrated my understanding of the Science of Mind. This would enable me to pass the practitioner's exam. My friend picked me up in her car, and we drove around the island, but I couldn't think of anything. Finally she stopped the car alongside the ocean in Waimānalo and said, "I'm not moving the car one inch until you give me an affirmation." I looked up at Mount Olomana and prayed silently, "If you have any power, give me an affirmation." I did this three times, then Mount Olomana spoke to me: "From the highest peak of my consciousness I look down upon the nothingness of things and see instead the beauty of God in all, for He is all." I told that to my friend. She asked me to repeat it, then drove me straight to a telephone and got Dr. Holmes on the line. When I repeated the affirmation to him, there was silence on the other end; he was very moved.

Ernest Holmes did not intend to start an organized church. He said, "You are Religious Science. I'm not." But others were insistent, and the last time I saw him was at the dedication of the Founder's Church in 1963. "Thank you for the two words you told the headquarters," he said. "I always did want to say it myself."

He was referring to an incident that had occurred during the years I gave treatments as a Science of Mind practitioner. One day in town I met a woman who had stopped coming for treatment. I asked her why she stopped. She said, "I have no money to pay you," and I responded, "Look at me! I'm Hawaiian. We give everything free." So I did not charge her the $10 practitioner's fee, and she told everybody about the Hawaiian woman giving her free treatments. Lots of other people came, and I gave them free treatments, too.

Eventually, I think, other practitioners wrote to the headquarters, and the headquarters reprimanded me, saying, "If you don't stop, we'll revoke your license." I took my license off the wall and mailed it back with a piece of paper with two words—"Shove it." Ernest Holmes thanked me for that the last time I saw him.

Dr. Holmes always impressed upon me, "Get a good metaphysical background, know God is all, and you will know who you are and what your potentials are. When you know that, you can go anywhere and have fellowship with anyone. But," he cautioned, "don't forget to meditate." I was deeply touched because he was giving me my freedom. Till this day, when I write, I feel that he is beside me.

Some time after I received my practitioner's license, my friend, whom I will call by the pseudonym Sheila, asked me to go to a seance with her. I told her I did not believe in seances, but she insisted, "Please come with me. My husband is on duty tonight." So I said, "How much?" She said, "Five dollars." I said, "You pay and I'll go."

So she paid, and I went, feeling like I was being a traitor to my own faith. The seance was held at the home of the famous *kahuna*, Daddy Bray, in Alewa Heights, a hillside neighborhood overlooking Honolulu. About 45 people were crowded into one room, and with the windows covered with curtains to shut out any light, it was like sitting in a steam bath. The medium went into a trance, and a spirit by the name of Susan took over. When the seance seemed to be ending without Sheila or me receiving any messages, Sheila got up and said, "Susan, you forgot me and Nana."

The spirit picked on me first, asking, "Nana, do you have a mother in the spirit world?" I poked my friend and said, "Shouldn't spooks know each other?" But I answered facetiously, "I have two. Which one is it?"

Susan said, "This one is named Mary." I said, "They were both Marys." All of a sudden another voice said to me, "Good evening, Nana, I have been with you all your life." Again I poked Sheila and whispered, "That's nonsense. My mother couldn't speak English. That spirit is speaking English to me." Then my natural mother, this spirit, said, "If I called you by your Hawaiian name, would you believe me?" I didn't say anything but thought, "My Hawaiian name is unusual. That would be the day if she called me by my name." The spirit started chanting and then said, "Lihilihipuamelekule." The lacy petals of the marigold blossom! *Nobody* knew my middle name. I had not used it since my natural mother died. So when I heard that, I cried. The next night I returned with my friend. This time I paid.

That second night, an Indian spirit came through and said to me, "We met on Sheila's screen door." He was talking about an incident that had happened some time before, one day when I was at Sheila's house, sitting on a couch with grandchildren crawling all over the floor. Suddenly I had heard a voice saying, "Who is this Indian?" I turned to Sheila, but she had not said anything. Yet three times I heard this question. The third time the voice was so forceful that I got up and looked around. Visible on the screen door was the image of an Indian man. I said, "Who is this Indian?" Sheila said, "What Indian? I don't see an Indian." But then for a fleeting second she saw him. In the second seance this Indian identified himself as Thundercloud, and I called him "Grandfather," Grandfather Thundercloud. Later I realized that he was my inner self. The spirit guide is our own inner being, actually a higher level of consciousness which we personalize to give it form. I called mine Grandfather Thundercloud and gave him an Indian face because I loved Indians as a child.

After that second seance, I begged, borrowed, and stole any book I could get on mediumship, and about a year later I became a medium myself. Thundercloud told me to begin. He acted as the doorkeeper that let the spirits come through me. Once St. Theresa came through. There was a scent of roses and all of a sudden a rain of rose petals. A Taoist scribe came through every week. During these seances my consciousness was among the stars, and only later would I find out what had happened.

Whenever we had a seance, we lit candles, and the candle flames rose to the ceiling as long as the seance lasted. We held meetings every week for two years, with the attendance eventually growing to around 50 people with some having to stand outside. One day the spirit said, "No more seances. Point people to God instead." So I stopped. We had had the experience of knowing about life after death, and it was time to move on.

Through Sheila I met Daddy Bray, who was her uncle. Although I never studied with him, Daddy Bray believed that I had the power. He wanted me to become his successor and insisted on initiating me as a *kahuna.* During the initiation, however, I had a friend and my son sit behind me with *ti* leaves, negating all that Daddy Bray was chanting.

One of the particular reasons Daddy Bray initiated me was to represent him at a gathering of the elders of the Hopi Indians in Arizona. I am told I was the first woman ever to go down into the *Kiva*, the chamber below the ground where the Hopi hold their sacred rituals. It was a powerful place. At first I sat against the wall, but Daddy Bray was projecting himself through me, and all of a sudden the elders came and brought me into their circle. They said they sensed Daddy Bray's presence here and wanted him in the circle when they passed the peace pipe.

At a dinner party Daddy Bray invited me to, I met a wealthy heiress who was to become an important part of my spiritual journey. I shall call her by the pseudonym Ruth. We sat directly across from each other at dinner but did not speak. Afterward, Sheila, who also had been at the dinner, still felt an urge to eat some Hawaiian food. We went back to my house, and while she was eating *poi*, all of a sudden, clairvoyantly, I saw a black dog, a German shepherd. Next to the dog I saw a round, black table with sloping edges and Chippendale legs. I told Sheila about the vision.

Three days later, Ruth had Daddy Bray call and invite me to her home near Diamond Head. At first I declined, but then he called Sheila, who finally persuaded me to go. We were ushered into the living room and served tea by the maid before Ruth came in and took us out to a pavilion by the sea. I took a chair next to the piano, while Sheila sat on the couch with Ruth. Abruptly Sheila called out, "Nana, Nana, the dog, the dog!"

"What dog?" I said, then "Oh, my God, that dog!" It was the black German shepherd I had seen three days earlier, and it was sitting next to that unusual table. The table, however, was white. After I told her my precognition, Ruth explained that the table had been bleached. She told me to take the table, but I didn't want it. She said to come and get it whenever I was ready, but the table is still there.

When Ruth invited me to fly to Seattle for more seances with the medium, I decided to go with her and eventually we became good friends. Subsequently I accompanied her on six trips around the world, our trips sometimes lasting for months. We spent extended periods in some places, so I got the feeling of really having lived in Paris, India, Thailand, London, and New York. These travels gave me a global perspective and made me feel like a citizen of the world.

Once, when we went to Cairo, an Egyptian tour agent was to show us the temples at Aswan, and he hired a car and driver to take us there. Going by car in Egypt is somewhat ridiculous because most of the country is the Sahara Desert. We drove through long stretches of desert broken only by little oases surrounded by mud huts. As the day wore on, our driver went faster and faster, as though somebody was pursuing him.

I had made it a habit to meditate when we rode on airplanes, trains, or cars. I started to meditate, and I heard Grandfather Thundercloud say, "Tell the driver to slow down. Your tires are going to blow out, and all of you will be killed." Looking up at the dashboard, I saw that we were going 90 miles an hour. The road was not good. I poked Ruth and said, "Tell the agent to tell the driver not to drive so fast because the tires are going to blow out and we're going to be killed." Ruth told the agent, but the driver said, "No! We're not going 90 miles an hour. The speedometer needs fixing. It says 90 but actually we're going 45." The agent turned around to look at us. I pointed straight at him: "You tell him to go slow." So the agent told him, "Slow down, you have to slow down."

Five minutes later, we were going bump, bumpety-bump, and the driver seemed not even to be aware of it. I nudged Ruth and said, "Doesn't he *know* that we have a flat tire?" Finally I poked the driver and told him. He said, "Wait a minute. We have a flat tire." He got out to fix it, but there was no spare. We had to turn around and drive 40 miles back to the nearest village. By the time we got there, the tire was wrapped around the rim and the axle.

Fortunately the village had tires and fuel, and we continued our trip only to discover that the driver did not know the way to Aswan. We lost the road at night and about two in the morning we drove up to an army barracks. The soldiers told us that the bridge ahead was out and suggested that we stop there until daylight. The driver went into the barracks. Ruth and I were extremely disgruntled, but we got some sleep in the car while the tour agent stood guard. At about five o'clock, the driver came and shook us awake: "Get up! Get up! Hurry up. We have to leave. Something happened." While we slept, an Egyptian woman had been murdered and decapitated 50 feet from our car. I said, "Thank you, God, for protecting us."

We piled into the car and left at the break of dawn. At a little village, we found a small inn where we decided to take a room, get something to eat, and freshen up. We were covered with dust from head to toe. I had bathed and just lain down and closed my eyes when Grandfather said, "Leave." I said, "What?" "You must leave now! Wake her up and leave *now*." I went to Ruth and woke her. "What's the matter?" she asked, "I'm tired."

"Too bad," I answered, "Grandfather says leave *now*." So we got into the car and drove off just before noon. We arrived in Luxor around five that afternoon. We rested and then picked up a paper to read while we sat drinking some lemonade. Big headlines announced that the inn that we had left had collapsed, killing two people inside.

My experiences in Science of Mind, in seances, and in different cultures all over the planet showed me what a mystical, metaphysical world we live in. Reality is not just what you know through physical senses or your education in one society and culture. The only way to know true reality is by going within.

God Loves You, I Love You

To me the concept of the "Beloved" conveys
not just a nice, cozy, warm relationship with God,
but one that is joyous, uplifting, and exhilarating
because it is a recognition of who I am.

In 1951, I started teaching metaphysics, first with senior citizens for 15 years and then with young people as well. I taught these classes for over 30 years, generally once a week whenever I was not traveling. What was most satisfying was seeing loners come in who were wrapped up in themselves; then all of a sudden they became part of the group. The group shared love with them.

A lot of people have asked, "What is metaphysics?" I like to say metaphysics is all about love. Love is an innate power you have within you that can change your life. Love is the nature of the inner self, your real self.

In Christianity, all of the laws that we must abide by have been resolved into two commandments. There were ten, but thank goodness now we have only two, and they are very beautiful. One says, "Thou shall love thy God with all thy heart, with all thy soul, with all thy strength, and with all thy mind." The second is, "Thou shall love thy neighbor as thyself." Love actually is a fulfillment of the law, and that simplifies everything. If you love others, you do not want to kill them or lie to them. Love is the key, and love is the law. It is love that releases us from all bondage of any kind.

Take, for example, a relationship problem where someone holds a grudge or animosity towards you. Appeal to the inner being, the God-nature that is within that person, to release him or her from negativity. We are not trying to change this individual; we are simply asking the spirit of God already within to come forth.

When this occurs, that person naturally lets go of resentment and animosity.

The only thing that can release anyone is love. Of course, it is difficult to love the person who resents you. But that is the true test of spiritual love, the only kind of love that is true and lasting. The scriptures say, "Love covers a multitude of sins." When you love someone, you do not see their faults, imperfections, and bad habits. You only see the God-nature within them. This takes a lot of work because we are creatures of habit, and through the years, we have personalized the shortcomings of others. To be impersonal is the perfect way. It does not mean that you shun others; it means that you rise above the shortcomings of others. You do not take their faults personally. You actually see people as wonderful, beautiful, healthy and, most of all, changing.

Many people are having problems with relationships, but all you have to do is turn around and pour more love into your relationship. I said this to someone, and she answered, "I already have." I said, "Well, not enough." She said, "I gave more than I possess." I said, "No, there is so much love inside of you; you haven't given half of what you have. You can never run out of love. Never! It's just that you don't want to love enough."

She came back later, cried, and said, "You know, Nana, I don't know how I ever can thank you. I tried and tried, and I finally broke through. I never thought it was going to be solved. I am so much happier that now I can relate not only to this person but to everybody." This is a spiritual kind of love.

When I say, "I love you," it is not I who really loves you; it's my inner self that loves you. The spiritual part of me is expressing itself for you. God is constantly making himself known to all of us, but we are so blind, we do not see it in the little things that people say to us, in the little happy moments we experience.

Although unconditional love is always what we really want, we are often afraid of love without consciously knowing it, and so we may act both blind and deaf to love's presence. "God is Love," the Scriptures tell us. As we help ourselves and each other to let go of fear, we begin to experience a personal transformation. We start to see beyond our old reality, as defined by the physical senses, and enter a state of clarity in which we discover that all minds are joined, that we share a common Self, and that inner peace and unconditional love are, in fact, real.

We can choose our own reality because our will is free. We can choose to see and experience the truth of our own reality as unconditional love. To do this, we must at each instant refuse to be limited by the fearful past and future, by the questionable "realities" we have accepted from our culture. We can choose to experience this instant as the only time there is and live a reality of *Now*.

Unconditional love is more than a sentiment. It is a deep sense of the goodness and the generosity of life. This love is the very essence of life, the creative principle behind everything—spiritually, emotionally, mentally, and physically—ever renewing, revitalizing, bringing joy, harmony, and blessings to everything and everyone it touches.

Love heals any kind of condition, whether it is physical, relational, or financial. Whatever it is, loves heals it. As long as we are filled with love for one another, we can help each other fulfill our purposes in life. Again, I am not talking about the human kind of love but rather the love which is all-embracing. As soon as you see something, you love it. You see this table. God created this table, not some man in China. That person was the instrument through which God was able to express himself and create a table.

Everything around us is God. We must feel and know this and appreciate the things that we have and appreciate the people in our own lives, all our friends, the gardener, the maid. Whoever it is, no matter what it is, it is God. We must become like Dr. Holmes, who looked at people walking down the sidewalk in Los Angeles and saw only God in so many faces. It is wonderful to be able to look at someone and say, "Well, look at God looking at me!"

In each of us, God is functioning through our physical body, and this is why we have to love the physical body and take care of it. This body is actually the temple of the holy spirit that is within us.

Quite some time ago, I had a habit of joining different religions just to have fellowship, and in this way I was introduced to Buddhism. For the most part the Buddhists did not teach me anything that I did not already know, but there was one thing I learned. Each member had a *butsudan*, a shrine which contained not the figure of the Buddha but rather a scroll with Japanese characters on it. One day, I asked, "What is that scroll in there?" One of the members very nicely looked at me and said, "That is the spiritual part of you that's hanging there." I looked at him and said, "Just a piece of paper with these Japanese characters on it? That's the spiritual part of me?"

In this sect, every morning when you get up you face east and say a prayer. Then you turn around, face the *butsudan*, and chant. One morning I had done the prayers and had turned to the *butsudan* when all of a sudden it dawned on me that the shrine itself was actually a symbol of my physical body, and the little scroll to which I was chanting was my inner self. That is what Buddhism taught me.

Now, every time I sit and meditate, it is easy for me to go within to this inner shrine. This body is the temple, and sitting here right in the center of my being is that spiritual part of me which is pure, which is never imperfect and which nothing can disturb. It is there holy, pure, and beautiful. This body is a shrine encasing this little, beautiful light that is within you. From this light come love and faith. This inner light within you makes all possible, but only if you believe it. It does not take any effort. Just believe. That is all you need to do. Just believe that there is God in the center within you, loving you, and all things are possible if you clear your channels by forgiving, by your personal practice of *ho'oponopono.*

In the Christian scriptures, Jesus says, "No man cometh unto the Father but by me," and so at the end of prayers, Christians all say, "In the name of Jesus Christ, we ask, amen." When Jesus made that statement, it was not Jesus himself who was speaking. It was the same part of each one of you that I am trying to help you develop and become more aware of; it was this God-nature or Christ-mind within him that was speaking.

When you are up in that level of consciousness, that Christ-mind, and speak your word, your prayer will be manifested. Direct your demand or prayer to the universal consciousness. Say it to God! Not to an individual, for there must be no intermediary—none! Prayer must be directed to deity as in the highest form of Christianity. Go directly to the source!

Can you close your eyes and pray to God and not see him as a being, as having form and shape? Can you do that? A lot of people, because of all of these pictures of Jesus, visualize God in human form. Whenever they pray to God, they see God looking like Jesus Christ or perhaps like an angry old man with a great white beard, sitting on a throne, holding a scythe in one hand and a scepter in the other. I don't believe in that kind of anthropomorphic God.

I know my God, the God that I talk to; my God is love. Because I feel and believe very strongly and very deeply, it is a force, a power. God is light. God is life. God is the spiritual energy in which we are immersed constantly. When we are inspired, we are absolutely free and open to the flow of universal energy. No matter what, we live, move, and have our being in Him. God is everything and so are you.

I want everyone to become aware of this: there is a part of yourself that you can speak to, that you can actually tell your secrets to. It will understand you and love you for it. Ernest Holmes said:

> I wish to impress upon you your nearness to this universal consciousness. Many persons feel so far away from God, and when they think of deity at all, they think of it as a being somewhere off in space. But God is difficult to reach only because you make it so with your wrong conceptions of your separateness from Him. You should take the great consciousness into every part and act of life. Whisper to it in the darkness of the night, and it will hear and answer you. See it in the darkness of the night, and it will hear and answer you. See it in a mental picture of golden yellow light, and it will fill your body with its uplifting vibrations. Depend upon it instead of persons and things to bring you what you need, and your demands will never fail to be met.

Cloud visiting the valley

Manifestation

Y ou are manifesting your life constantly. You manifest your experiences from thoughts and feelings which have sunk down into the subconscious mind. You can manifest your highest good if you recognize your divinity. As I said before, we are co-creators with God. God and ourselves are not separate. This is why we say the Father within, not the Father up there; it is always the Father within. God and ourselves are a unity beyond dualism.

In the "Laws of Manifestation" Ernest Holmes wrote that there are four levels: first the physical, the mental, the emotional, and finally the soul. The soul level is what I talk about mostly. The physical level is something we experience only for a short while. The soul level is a permanent thing. When changes happen at this level, they manifest themselves on all other levels.

Let's say a person is very, very ill, and the doctor says, "This disease cannot be cured." Such a person must turn away from the doctor's diagnosis and turn to God alone. And where is God? Here! Right here, within. So you turn to that perfection that is within you, and as you become aware of it, it begins to express itself through you. It comes out as perfect health.

The first thing you must do is clear your channels. Whenever anything negative is happening to you, your channels are blocked with negative thought patterns. These blocks do not allow positive thought patterns to function through you. This is why we must meditate. When you meditate, you are forgiving everyone and clearing your channels. If you are not demonstrating anything, not bringing into manifestation the things that you want in your life, then the channels are blocked. What are the channels? The way you think and the way you feel about things, people, and events in your life—in short, your consciousness.

It is not worth harboring any kind of resentment. Life is too short. You want to lead a happy life unhampered by illnesses and negative experiences. Do you know that it takes more energy to be negative than to be positive? It takes more energy to worry about something than to actually look at the problem. It takes more energy to be angry, to be worried, to be hateful than to be loving, considerate and respectful. Scientists have found out that every time we become angry or resentful, we shorten our lives. It is not worth it.

When we do not learn from a negative experience, it becomes increasingly painful. It hurts so much after a while that you grow numb to it. A mental callus grows over the hurt, and eventually you become absolutely numb to it. It does not seem to affect you, but it is leaving scars in the subconscious mind. It is not hurting now, but it is going to hurt later on.

You must dissolve these hurts and scars with love. One of the laws of manifestation is that when you start loving from the soul, from the inner part of you, you unblock all of your channels. Every channel is unblocked just through that love.

When the channels are clear, we recognize one Presence, one Life, one Intelligence, one Substance, and we identify ourselves with It. The energies or vibrations flow freely. Infinite intelligence flows through you and gives you ways to manifest your ideas as long as you are relaxed and receptive. But the minute you get excited, tense, and rigid, nothing works. Ernest Holmes called manifestation "a relaxed, effortless endeavor."

After the channels are clear, we must affirm our highest good. Affirmations put your thoughts into words, and words have power. Most of us make statements without even thinking. If you catch yourself saying, "I'm sick and tired," immediately erase or cancel that remark because otherwise you are going to manifest being sick and tired. Whenever I even hear anything negative, I negate the words. I refuse to accept the negative remarks. They interfere with my positive thoughts.

When you make an affirmation, be careful about your choice of words and about how definite your declaration of the desired good is. Most importantly, you must feel the words you are saying. You must accept intellectually and emotionally that they are so. Affirming is to declare, not to supplicate. Ernest Holmes wrote, "You are declaring something as true, affirming the reality of the good you desire. It is a demand which you are making on the Universe, which, according to its nature, has no choice other than to fulfill the demand according to the nature of the demand."

A student once asked me how to get a job. I told him to affirm with me, "I'm one with the Father in whom I live and move and have my being. I now move into my right place." He worked with me that day, and when he left, I told him, "Call me as soon as you get a message." Next morning at 9:30 he phoned and said, "Mrs. Veary, you're a witch." "Did you say bitch or witch?" I asked. He said, "You're a witch. I got hired on a job at a television station." I said, "Thank you, Father."

Three weeks later, my daughter told me that this student had been promoted at a radio station. He called me to say, "Mrs. Veary, I'm so glad I have you." I told him, "You better not believe that. I'm not the one who did it. You did it yourself. Just go to meet your highest good today." This is the way it should be for all of us. Affirm that all the channels to our highest good are open and that God blesses us according to our needs, to the extent that we can embrace His gifts.

Work silently on your affirmations. When you talk about them, you deplete the energy you need to bring them into manifestation and open yourself to the skepticism of others. If you need it, however, a practitioner of Science of Mind can boost your faith. The practitioners can meditate on lifting your consciousness up—that is all—from there on, you are on your own. Otherwise, how can I say you did it all by yourself?

My favorite affirmation is: I now let God's greatness manifest in me. All power is instantly available at every point in space and every instant of time. I know this, and all fear is erased from my consciousness. I join with all those who know God as the only Power and Presence in their lives. God in me is my resource, and nothing can harm me. I know that I am the cause of my experiences. Love attends me wherever I go. Peace envelops me at every moment. The more I know of God, the less I create or experience difficulties. I steadfastly watch my thoughts. I consecrate my consciousness to Truth. The endless possibilities of life are before me, and nothing can prevent my full spiritual development. I know that I am growing in spiritual and factual demonstrations. I am the victorious creation of God, and I triumph in all my ways. I live with ease, for my thinking is right and my world responds to my decisions. I am fully conscious that my word eliminates every bondage, whether in myself or others. I claim good judgment. I claim the integrity of God as mine, today.

After clearing your channels and affirming your desired good, the last step is accepting. Dr. Holmes said, "The gift is always given but awaits our acceptance of it." He suggested that we affirm, "I now accept the creative action of the words I have spoken as law. They go forth into immediate fulfillment right now. Nothing can prevent them from being fully and completely fulfilled in my experience." Give thanks even before receiving the blessing.

Let me give you an example of a manifestation. Once I overheard my son-in-law and my daughter talking about some financial reverses. It bothered me. I was worried about my grandchildren. So that night before I went to bed, I prayed and affirmed that I would demonstrate a certain amount of money. When I got up, it was the first thing on my mind. I affirmed again that all the channels were open and that I would be led to my highest good. I thanked the Father, knowing I had already received it.

I asked my daughter to take me down to the bank. She said, "What do you want to go for? To rob the bank?" She poked fun at me, but I was in that high consciousness so it did not bother me. I said, "I just want to go to the bank." She said, "Oh, my goodness, Mama! Do you have a bank account?" I said, "No, just take me to the bank." Finally she agreed.

As we headed out the door, something told me to take a brown paper bag. I said to myself, "What's a brown paper bag for?" But I had to listen. If it told me to take a gunny sack, I would have taken a gunny sack. I went back in and came out with a paper bag. When I got into the car, my daughter said, "Now, Mother, you're not going to put that over your head when you walk into the bank, are you?" I did not say anything.

We drove to the bank, but she said, "I'm not going to park in front of the bank." She parked in front of another store, and I had to walk. It did not matter: I felt as if I was being led; I was so sure of what I was doing that nothing bothered me. It almost seemed routine or mechanical.

I walked in and told a teller I wanted to borrow a thousand dollars. She called the manager, and he took me to his desk to fill out a form. I read the form, which asked me about my occupation, property, bank accounts, and so on. I looked at the form and said to myself, "Well, Grandfather, you brought me here." I filled out my name, address, and birthdate. For occupation, I put "none!" Checking account, none! Savings account, none!

The manager came back, looked at the form, and said, "Oh, you're Mrs. Veary." I said, "Yes." He said, "Fine. How do you want it? Do you want it in a checking account?" I said, "No, I want cash." He got the money, counted it all out, and asked, "Is there anything else I can do for you?" I said, "Oh, no, thank you very much." Then the paper bag came in handy. I put all the money inside and walked out of the bank.

As soon as I was out, I panicked. "Oh, no!" I said to myself, "Grandfather, you brought me here, and you'll have to pay this back. You know very well I don't work. Where am I going to get a thousand dollars to pay this bank back?" It seemed like something said to me firmly, "Be still!" So I composed myself and walked to the car. When my daughter saw the money, she said, "What? You held up the bank?"

Three days later, the mailman brought a check for $8,000 which was a finder's fee for some property I had located for a foundation. I hurried back to the bank to see the manager. He could not remember me, but I told him that he had given me the loan form. He found the document in his files, and as he scanned it and saw his own signature approving the loan, his eyes grew big with surprise. He said, "I did this? You didn't fill out anything." I paid him back, and we have been friends ever since.

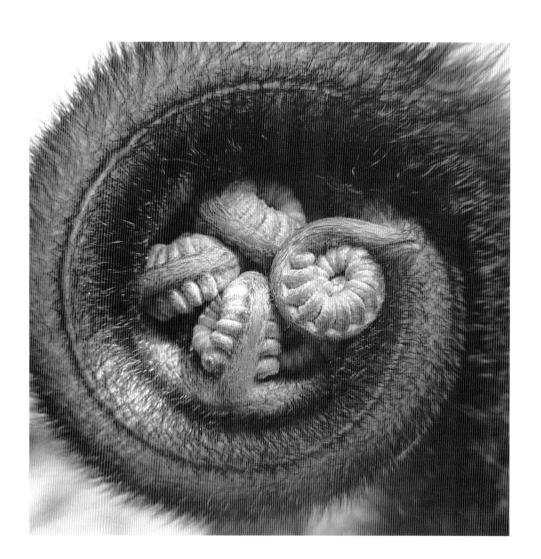

Changes

Repentance reaches fullness when you are brought to gratitude for your mistakes.

I do my counseling over breakfast at Michel's, a lovely French restaurant on the beach at Waikiki. I let the waves wash the problems out to sea. When I am called upon for counseling, the first thing I do is meditate and rise in consciousness. In meditation one tries to lift the client's consciousness up and out of the problem so that the client can see it objectively. Both the solution and the problem lie in the client's consciousness.

The second thing I do is to skip the details. The details of the problem and of the client's personal life are none of my business. My concern is purely spiritual. I can support the client's positive objectives, but the rest the client must do himself or herself. I tell people who are suffering with a problem, "Just let it go! If you have a hot coal in your hand, you just let it go. You don't analyze the situation; you just let it go."

We generally do not think about changes until they happen. Then we often are upset because we are comfortable in old situations and wary of new ones. But everything changes: your activities, your thoughts, your jobs, your relationships. If we do not allow these changes to take place, we work against the flow of life and suffer negative experiences that are really hard to cope with. If we let go, then changes happen gracefully. I have gone from the ways of old Hawai'i to the Pentecostal faith to spiritualism and then to metaphysics, but I never felt like I had to make a difficult choice to change. Each change happened naturally as part of the spiritual journey I have been on all my life.

Letting go in personal relationships can be the most difficult, a true test of your spiritual strength. For instance, my son is past 50, and I still mother him. The other night, however, when someone asked me, "Are you Emma Veary's mother?" I finally could say, "No, I'm not her mother anymore. I'm her friend." There are also children who find it difficult to release their parents and to go out on their own. Both must release the other. Children must go out and must make mistakes because this is the way they grow. This is what gives strength of character. In a romantic relationship, letting go can be even harder. If I am in love with somebody, and the other party wants to change the nature of the relationship, the one who is holding back *must* release. Many people suffer because they hold tight at this time of change.

Sometimes tragic changes happen inadvertently and unexpectedly. These can be truly heart-breaking changes. When Jesus said, "Watch ye and pray," he meant it. I encourage every one of you to pray and meditate every morning because sudden tragedy can take your health or the life of someone you love. This is why you cannot separate yourself from God. You live, move, and have your being in God, and you need Him.

Sometimes we have to make changes that we do not like and we tend to procrastinate on these. This was one of the hardest habits I had to overcome. In my younger days I could procrastinate for months, but not anymore. Whatever you must change at any particular time, change! When it comes into your awareness, that is the appointed time, the right time for you to change, the time when you will get its full benefits.

It may be that you are not prepared to change because you have not evaluated the situation. You must ask yourself, "What am I getting out of this experience? If I were to make this decision, would it help me to grow? Would it bring me more happiness? If I stay the way I am, what will happen? Am I resisting change because I am afraid or too comfortable?"

In the end, the right decision is spiritually inspired by the inner self. In the end, love guides you to make the right decision. A decision may lead to an awful lot of trouble, but do not regret it. It was meant to be. The problems you experience contribute to your spiritual growth. When you learn the lesson of these experiences, the situation will change again. Until you do, although you may want it to change badly, the situation will remain as it is.

For instance, once I lived in a townhouse, but I could not accept it. I found all kinds of excuses: "I've never lived in an apartment or townhouse before. I'm not used to hearing people talking or toilets flushing through the walls." I put my name on a waiting list for a condominium that would be quieter and was told that my apartment would be ready in no time. Months passed, but nothing happened until I learned the lesson of that townhouse. Once I did, I was released and could go on to the next experience.

The change people fear most is death, but this is a needless fear. We are God, wearing a garment of flesh. When we get through our time on Earth, we must shed this body because it is too gross to carry further. We have to drop it just like taking our clothes off. We came with nothing, and we leave with nothing.

I was talking about this one day in a class my son happened to attend. After everyone left, he said, "Mother, you should be arrested for saying things like that." I said, "What are you talking about?" He continued, "You really should be arrested.

You make death sound so beautiful I feel like going out and committing suicide. What am I doing here if it is so beautiful? Who wants to be around here with all of the worries, fears, doubts, and what have you? You shouldn't go around talking to people about death like that!" But that is exactly what death is like. It is not something to be feared. It is just like changing clothes.

My children once told me they were very concerned about me. I said, "For goodness sake! I don't want you kids to worry about me. I'm fine! When you worry about me, you're keeping me from growing spiritually. I'm going to send it right back to you." They said, "But Mother, we don't want anything to happen to you like it did to Dad." I said, "Don't worry. I've already ordered my way of departing this earth." My children said, "What do you mean?" I said, "When I say good-night to you, I just might be saying good-bye."

When friends who have not seen me for a long time ask me what I have been doing, I tell them, "I'm getting ready for my next trip." When you get to my age, what else do you do? If you know very well you have a trip to make, you had better get ready for it.

But, life is so beautiful that everyday I am deeply thankful. When I wake up in the morning, I stretch in bed, and as soon as I open my eyes, I say, "Thank you, Father, for this new day which means a new beginning for me."

You create the changes in your life through your thoughts. Thought is a vibration and therefore a force. Thought is energy, the creative medium that you use to manifest the experiences of your life. To think is to create. Because of thought, we are co-creators with God. If you are not aware of your thinking, then unconsciously you are bringing experiences into your life that you may not want. You must become aware of your thoughts and ask yourself, "Is this a creative thought? How is it creative? Is it going to create something negative?" Dr. Holmes said, "Thought is neither good nor bad, but like any other force, the use of it determines its character." Just remember that, whether you are conscious of it or not, you are using an energy.

I do not believe that there is such a place as heaven or hell. I believe that we create the happiness of our own heaven or the misery of our own hell. We create all the experiences that we go through; all of them come from the subconscious mind. Thoughts and feelings sink down into the subconscious and emerge as experiences—sooner or later. The thoughts of today are your experiences of tomorrow.

It is important not to give negative thoughts any feeling because the feeling empowers the thought. The feeling opens the lid to the subconscious mind. The stronger the feeling, the deeper the thought seed sinks into the subconscious. Then the lid closes, and the thought begins to take form and emerge in your experience. If the thought is negative, you suffer from it. If it is positive, your experience is beautiful. Generally, though, whenever something is positive, you do not give it the kind of strong feeling that you do when something is negative. Compare the times when you are happy to when you get so damn angry.

The subconscious mind is the house of memory. Everything is there. To show you how the subconscious mind works, let me tell you about an experience I had. When I was around five or six, my mother took me to a *lu'au* at the Kapi'olani Maternity Home. Like all children at big social functions, eventually I got bored and tired. I cried and nagged at my mother, whining, "I want to go home. I want to go home. I'm tired." My mother sat me down on the grass and said, "We cannot go home. The *lu'au* is for all the babies who were born here." I said, "Well, why did I have to come?" She said, "You were born here."

When I was 50, my daughter went to Kapi'olani to give birth to my granddaughter Debbie. I was sitting in the waiting room, when all of a sudden my attention was drawn to a sign over the door. I kept looking at it. I just saw the word, "Records," and in a flash, I had a vision of a little girl, me, with my mother on the grass. I could see it as vividly as though it were happening at that moment. Can you imagine the subconscious spewing this out from way down deep inside, from the time I was five years old? I had never thought about it before.

Where do ideas come from? Not from you. When you have an idea, it is not your idea. These ideas are all from the infinite intelligence that floats around in the ether here. These ideas are all there, and it is up to you to reach out.

For instance, once when I had a job designing women's clothes, my colleague and I were in a rush to complete a whole line of dresses for a fashion show. One day she was making coffee and grabbed the pot directly, almost burning her hand. So she used a dish towel as a potholder, and 15 or 20 minutes later an idea came to mind. "Hmm!" I said, "Wouldn't it be wonderful to design a mitten that could be used as a potholder." This type of mitten had not been invented yet. My friend said, "What?!" I said, "A mitten! You know, we could make mittens that are potholders." She said, "How could we do that?" I said, "Well, we could get all these scraps together that are lying around and sew them up like a quilt. If we padded it, we could use it for a pot holder." The idea was terrific. We talked about it, but we did not do anything about it because we were too involved with this line of dresses we were trying to get out on time.

After the fashion show, the idea just faded out of our lives. We forgot it entirely until, about a year later, we were at a department store and saw potholder mittens, exactly what we had thought of doing. That idea did not require any capital at all. All you had to do was get scraps from the garment factory and sew them up. Somebody else picked the idea up because we were too lazy to follow through. That person got a royalty for every mitten that was manufactured and is a multi-millionaire today. Can you imagine?

Now where did the idea come from? This is why we have to be very alert mentally. Ideas come with the means. But we never bothered because we felt, "What's a silly little mitten compared to all of these dresses we're creating?" Once the line was out, we had the fashion show, the buyers sent their orders, and that was it! We got paid for it, and that was the end of the line. But this mitten would have gone on and on. If we had patented it, we would have received a royalty for every mitten manufactured. After the seventh year, the idea is open to the public, but by that time we would have been wealthy.

But maybe we were not meant to be wealthy. The point here is not to pooh-pooh the thoughts that come to your mind. Study every thought that comes to mind. Remember, all the channels to the infinite intelligence are always entirely open for you if you affirm that these channels are open.

The will is the engine which powers thoughts into creations. Will is a tremendous force. In its higher aspects it is latent in most people and must be awakened. Like the muscles of the body it grows stronger with use. Each of you determines whether you remain infirm of purpose and weak in will or arouse this force and use it for your bidding. A *kahuna 'ana'ana*, or Hawaiian shaman, used his will to accomplish the desired results of his religious practice.

Breakfast at Michel's

The will determines the intensity of a thought, the feeling behind the thought. Without feeling, there is no intensity; without intensity, there is no feeling. If the will is strong, the thoughts will travel a long distance. This is what we use for absent treatment. For someone who is ill far away, it is not necessary to jump on a plane and fly over there. All you have to do is sit very quietly, go into meditation, and affirm that person's perfection no matter how bad the illness or the accident. If you sit down very quietly and visualize the person as being completely whole, perfect, and willing to do the manifestation, immediately that person will feel it on the other side of the ocean.

We have something to work on, something to work with! God put us on this earth-plane completely equipped to have a happy and fulfilled life. Because we have not used our potential to the utmost, we are as we are today. *We should be much more advanced mentally, much more evolved spiritually, and much more prosperous! To be prosperous is God's law!* You are meant to be prosperous.

No one can hope to become prosperous, healthy and wise without cultivating the will. The will forms the mental mold, in order that the mind may draw to itself whatever it desires through meditation. Meditation is an alert and receptive condition of mind, assumed for the purpose of receiving knowledge of a selected subject from the infinite intelligence.

Never, under any circumstances, permit yourself to use your will in a negative manner. The moment you become negative you become subject to entities and influences which may control or obsess you and perhaps dominate your mind throughout this life. The minute you find yourself negative, immediately jump on the positive side. Immediately become positive! Even if you have only a penny in your pocket, still thank God for that penny.

Changes

This is my affirmation for change: I unloose the wellsprings of my being and make a complete deliverance of the self to Life. This I do with joy, withholding nothing. I have no hope of reward. Everything I have belongs to the world. In giving, I shall receive the world back into my consciousness.

I let go of all prejudice and fixed opinions. I am willing to see God's action in every man. I pass no judgments, and I refuse all finalities. I open my whole being to changes for the better. I also allow everyone around me to change and enjoy new experiences in life. This is the joy of living.

I let life move me forward into greater joy. There are no anchors in my world to fasten me to any one situation. I accept the ever-changing, ever-unfolding action of God in my experience. I appreciate the past, but it cannot bind me to any person, place, or thing. No more weeping for what might have been. Today is the day of glory, and tomorrow is alive with the possibilities of creative self-expression. My consciousness is cleansed and awaits all new ideas with expectancy. These ideas will take me out of the present into the heaven of fresh conditions.

I let changes take place in my life. I know they must, and I know they *will!* I accept all change as a spiritual adventure and begin the discovery of God in every new condition. I find the treasure of the kingdom of God buried in all men and its coffers overflowing with kindness. I break all chains which bind me and walk free into God's great experience of life.

Hawaiian petroglyph

Forest at Kōkeʻe

Silent Retreats

You are made whole again in
silence. Solitude shatters the illusion
that you and I are separate.

About eight years ago, I stopped giving classes in metaphysics and began holding silent retreats. I changed my emphasis from talking to God in prayer to listening to Him in silence. In silent retreats which last several days, you can go deeply into your consciousness. The purpose is to free yourself of anger, guilt, resentment, discouragement, disappointment, worry, all the negative thought patterns buried in the subconscious mind. In silent retreats you clear your channels so life can be fulfilled. Silent retreats give you spiritual dignity.

We retreat from the outside world to go within to the very center of our being to acquaint ourselves with our spiritual counterpart. Usually this counterpart has been totally neglected and ignored. Wadsworth Emerson wrote, "The purpose of Life seems to be to acquaint man with himself. The highest revelation is the realization that God is in every man."

When we arrived on this planet, we were thoroughly equipped with the intelligence to know right from wrong, with the creative mind to invent the comforts we are enjoying today, with the wisdom to live life joyously and to the fullest, and with love to sustain us. In all this, God is expressed through us. We are to recognize and acknowledge that we are spiritual beings, living in the awareness of who and what we are—powerful beings. To recognize, "to know again," our divinity means to acknowledge that we are spiritual beings above all and to accept it.

My favorite place to hold retreats is Kōke'e on the Hawaiian island of Kaua'i. Kōke'e is a lush, forested park at an elevation of 4,000 feet, overlooking the Napali coast. It is Nature in silent grandeur. In Kōke'e the trees flex their muscles when I pass by. The place has powerful energies. Every time we go to Kōke'e, all the students' lives are turned around. They might not know it immediately, but later, all of a sudden they say, "I feel different," and they remember my talks.

At these retreats we gather twice a day for meditation, at sunrise and after sunset. I give a short talk following the meditation, and after the evening talk, we have dinner together. I tell them, "Walk in silence among the tall trees, cool streams, and sunny ridges. Meditate with plants and rocks to get some answers. Feel the healing power of the Earth as you reconnect with your spirit in the beauty of nature. Feel the

heartbeat of the Earth. Learn the beauty of walking with the rhythm of the Earth and opening your senses to receive new sounds and sensations. Experience the power of being alive in the present moment." Besides this, I have no instructions for people to get into the silence. I leave it to them and spend most of my time reading and writing beside the cabin window. On the last day, as the sun rises, we break the silence at the top of the Kalalau Lookout.

Silence means no repetitions, no affirmations, no denials, only a conscious acknowledgment of God's allness. In the silence, one is beyond words and thoughts. The deeper the silence, the more powerful the meditation. One's spiritual experiences in the silence are to be kept holy and sacred. The more we keep it secret and

sacred, the greater the power, and there you have the mystic!

In silence the conscious thinking mind comes to a stop, and the invisible presence and power are given the opportunity to function. If we really believe that the kingdom of God is within, we should be willing to leave the world until such time as we can reach, touch, and respond to the Father within.

Silence was the secret of the power of the Hawaiians. Through silence they communicated with nature. The language of silence salutes the divinity in all living things. Everything that has life has something of value to share with us, providing we are ready to experience it. Everything responds to us at the level of our recognition and acceptance of it. William James, the trailblazing American psychologist, said, "All nature awaits our recognition, acceptance, and cooperation with it."

All that God is, is around us and within us and eternally asking us to recognize it. We must learn to see the possibility of God rather than the impossibilities that the world believes in. Our security lies in this ability to *know* truth regardless of conditions and to know love regardless of hurts. There may be impossibilities today, but God is my eternal possibility of unlimited good, infinite love, and perfect health.

Those who live without spiritual vision and understanding are forever trying to solve problems by manipulating their human minds and exerting their human wills. This does not work in the end because all problems begin and end with the individual's own consciousness. As we realize that God's Mind is the basis of our individual consciousness, we begin to solve our problems at their point of origin, which is within ourselves.

We enter the silence through meditation. The highest form of meditation is inner stillness. In meditation, let your mind and heart release all that disturbs you. Let your body and all that surrounds it be still. Let the earth and sea and air and heaven itself be still. Think of Spirit as streaming, pouring, rushing, and shining into you, through you, and out from you in all directions while you sit quietly. Life is lived from inside out. You are a dynamic center in the creative flow that is God.

Meditation is the art of listening. When you pray, you are talking to God. When you meditate, you are listening to God. A beautiful scripture says, "Be still and know that I am God." When you meditate, you tune into the universal mind by being very still, but do not become passive. Be absolutely alert. You are not in meditation to sleep. You are in meditation for inspiration and spiritual unfoldment.

In meditation, after a period of contemplation, we rise in consciousness into an atmosphere of receptivity, into a consciousness where miracles take place. We come to a place of transition where Truth leaves the mind and enters the heart. Truth is no longer an intellectual knowledge about "Truth," but rather a living thing within our own being. With a change of consciousness, we *are* Truth.

Meditation is an uninhibited, unconditional movement of the individual consciousness in harmony with the rhythm of the universal life. The importance of meditation, or inner prayer, cannot be emphasized enough. We must take a few minutes daily to acknowledge the source of our being—God within. We should make a daily practice of meditation every morning and every sunset to keep us aware of our divinity, our spiritual counterpart. The world, this planet, is undergoing tremendous changes. If you do not meditate and get in touch with your spiritual self, you will be the loser.

Separation from the source leads to deterioration. Anything or anyone separated from the source begins to deteriorate mentally and physically and dies spiritually. The "light" goes out. We are light, don't you know? The Scriptures tell us, "Ye are the light of the world."

Yet we stumble around in the dark. We create confusion and label it evil or call it the demon. Neither exists in reality. We create our own evil and demons. We are co-creators with God, and in this case we are using the God-power wrongly. We have separated from the source and mistakenly invested confused thoughts with a power they do not have.

We need to "repair the broken communication" within ourselves. We must be honest with ourselves, forgive ourselves, get back in touch with the source, and all will be well. We can do it all by ourselves. In silence we can.

Walk in silence among the tall trees

Nana with Tanouye Roshi

Aloha at Chozen-ji

When Alvin Shim took me to Chozen-ji, International Zen Dojo in Kalihi Valley, and introduced me to Tanouye Tenshin Roshi, I felt like I had come home to the end of my journey. My first meeting with Roshi was just wonderful. I had the expectation that I was going to meet a Buddhist dressed in priestly robes. Instead, I met a man who was natural and comfortable in his coveralls. From the clothing, you could not tell who was the master and who were the monks. There was no pretense about Tanouye Roshi. I immediately fell in love with him.

When we were ready to leave, Roshi looked at me compassionately and said to Al, "I want her to lie down." I said, "Lie down where?" Roshi said, "Down on the floor." When I was on the floor, he treated me, holding my feet and putting energy back into my body. When he did this on another occasion, I saw the fluorescent lights get brighter. Little particles of energy were floating around. I felt light, as if I was floating. When he was finished, he hit the bottom of my feet and my hands, saying, "That's to prevent any leaks. Now you're good for another 100,000 miles."

Tanouye Roshi told me, "You came here half in and half out. You wanted to check out." I felt naked because he had read my mind. He said, "We need you. There's a lot of work for you to do." Roshi gave me his *rakusu* (bag) and a fan at that first meeting.

Roshi is wonderful. He is one in a million. All the people are fortunate to have

Roshi because he is wise, spiritual, and humorous. When I see Roshi today, I see a different person than the person I first met. In the beginning when I hugged him, he did not hug back, but now he hugs back.

Tanouye Roshi is one I can talk with; he understands me. He talks about the Hawaiians compassionately and helped me understand how we must change. Hawaiians are not defined by their blood. Hawaiians are those who have the spirit of aloha. In this sense, all of us must become Hawaiians.

It delights me to hear Tanouye Roshi talk about aloha. He also worked with Pilahi Paki, who was a wonderful person and teacher, and at the temple is a poster with Pilahi's description of the aloha spirit:

> "Aloha Spirit" is the coordination of mind and heart...it's within the individual. It brings you down to yourself. You must think and emote good feelings to others.
>
> A   stands for *akahai*, meaning kindness, to be expressed with tenderness.
> L   stands for *lokahi*, meaning unity, to be expressed with harmony.
> O   stands for *'olu'olu*, meaning agreeable, to be expressed with pleasantness.
> H   stands for *ha'aha'a*, meaning humility, to be expressed with modesty.
> A   stands for *ahonui*, meaning patience, to be expressed with perseverance.

When I saw this poster, I felt I had come full circle. From the aloha of old Hawai'i, I went to love and faith in the Pentecostal tradition, to spiritualism and world travels, to the metaphysics of Science of Mind, and finally to Chozen-ji and a Zen master who taught aloha.

I love going to *sesshin* at Chozen-ji. *Sesshin* means "to collect the mind" and is a five-day period of intensive meditation. *Zazen*, the meditation practice, brings the mind to a stop and permits the higher self to function. The purpose of *sesshin* and silent retreats is the same: to still the mind and realize one's True Self. I have been to *sesshin* at Chozen-ji six times. Each was beautiful. When we meditated, I felt we all joined forces to rise in consciousness.

For many years now my life has been simple. I hold silent retreats, enjoy myself at Chozen-ji, give blessings, counsel people, and write. Let me end with my latest reflections.

To me, these are the qualities of a spiritual life:

1. Unconditional love radiating as pure joy. A person is so filled with love and the joy of living that he or she naturally repels anything negative.
2. Peace. Knowing that tension will close the door to goodness, a spiritually awake person lives in a center of serenity regardless of what is going on outside him.
3. Right judgment. As people move into spiritual consciousness, their common sense is transformed into spiritual wisdom. Locking onto the spirit within, spiritually attuned people follow every prompting of their intuitions.
4. The presence of God. A spiritual person practices the art of self-awareness and works with God as co-creator.

The scriptures say, "Judge not, that you be not judged." There is only one Self, the eternal I Am. If you condemn someone or something, you condemn yourself, your own Being. If you forgive, you give to yourself.

"Forgive and you shall be forgiven." Forgiving means to set everyone and everything fully free, to release them totally within your own being, realizing that in Being you are not dependent on anyone or anything, and they are not dependent on you.

In forgiving, you give up the illusion of the separate ego, the illusion of dualism. The ego tries to possess every person, condition, and thing it comes into contact with. Ego is the false sense of self which arises when the higher law of being is broken. When you seek to possess someone or something, you bind yourself. Free yourself in consciousness. You alone bind yourself, and you alone can free yourself.

This truth is expressed in Kahlil Gibran's *The Prophet*:

> *Love one another, but make not a bond of love:*
> *Let it rather be a moving sea between the shores*
> *   of your souls.*
> *Fill each other's cup but drink not from one cup.*
> *Give one another of your bread but eat not from*
> *   the same loaf.*
> *Sing and dance together and be joyous, but let*
> *   each one of you be alone,*
> *Even as the strings of a lute are alone though*
> *   they quiver with the same music.*
> *Give your hearts, but not into each other's*
> *   keeping.*
> *For only the hand of Life can contain your*
> *   hearts.*
> *And stand together yet not too near together:*
> *For the pillars of the temple stand apart,*
> *And the oak tree and the cypress grow not in*
> *   each other's shadow.*[1]

1. Kahlil Gibran, *The Prophet* (New York: Alfred Knopf, 1976), pp. 15-16.

Working spiritually is the only thing that satisfies me. Unfortunately, today many people are work-aholics at making money and have lost sight of the spiritual nature of our work. Since all is God, whether our work be at home or in business, it is God's work if we only let God unfold through us. This requires a constant reminder to our egos that the inner self, born of God, will work through us if we let it. The Holy Spirit working through man always moves toward perfection.

Dr. Holmes said, "God in man, as man, *is man.*" Sai Baba says, "We are Gods!" Knowing their own vices and weaknesses, people have difficulty accepting this and forget the spiritual part of their identity. Therefore, how different we are from the avatars, messiahs, and divine messengers who recognize their descent from God and accept their own divinity.

A few have a vision that calls to the world to reawaken the spiritual nature of human beings and human society. Within all patterns of instability, forces struggle to achieve dominance. Yet beneath it all, a profound planetary spirit of love and good will is at work.

Truth is simple! To quote Wadsworth Emerson, "Whenever a mind is simple and receives Divine Wisdom, old things pass away. Means, teachers, texts, and temples fall. Truth lives now and absorbs past and future into the present."

Jesus was not interested in the logics of theology. He was primarily concerned with the spirit of humankind. There is an interior Christ-Mind that baffles all reasoning and is beyond all human explanation. Whence I have come is of little importance. Where I will go I am willing to leave to the wisdom of the Father. The Divine is a perfect simplicity. Life flows through me, love seeks an outlet from me, and power is mine to use as I select.

My use of the spirit is not dependent upon my education, social background, or theological beliefs. God in me acts through me as I recognize Him. I no longer seek an outside God. I have a simplified concept of God.

All things evolve from nothingness. According to our thought patterns, we give it form. You suffer because you believe your world to be real and solid. See it for what it really is: God's expression! Your body has no existence of its own. The five principles of matter, senses, cognition, will, and consciousness are vanities feeding your ego. Because you are a co-creator with God, you create an illusory world according to these principles and mistake it for reality. The true essence of reality is God. Only God exists.

Reality is the same yesterday, today, and forever. It is wonderful to know that something permanent, substantial, and eternal stands in the midst of our being and watches with joy the eternal changes taking place. To the spirit, these changes are merely variations of the experience of Mind. Everything that we now experience objectively will change, as it ought to, but that which is God abideth! This "I am," which is God within me, is substantial, changeless, and perfect.

The consciousness of God in the human soul is the essence, the sum and substance of all religion. It is the essence of the teachings of all the seers and mystics in the world's history. To become centered in God Consciousness is the first essential of every satisfactory life. The second is to go out thinking, speaking, working, loving, living from this center to serve God in others. Service is the greatest principle of practical ethics.

Sam Foss's "The House by the Side of the Road" expresses my feelings about my life:

> *...Let me live in a house by the side of the*
>   *road,*
> *Where the race of men go by.*
> *The men who are good and the men*
>   *who are bad,*
> *As good and as bad as I.*
> *I would not sit in the scorner's seat*
>   *or hurl the cynic's ban;*
> *Let me live in a house by the side of the*
>   *road and be a friend to man....*[2]

2. Sam Foss, *Best Loved Poems of All Time,* ed. Gail Harano (Kansas City: Hallmark Cards, 1968), p. 46.